Contents

Director's Foreword

There are several stages to the judging process, which unfolds over two days. The first stage involves viewing all the entries sequentially and allowing the most telling or effective to be set aside and to be looked at again. The portraits are judged anonymously and there must be something powerful in the portrait itself (whatever the type or style) for it to win through. During the second stage there is more debate, as judges test out their various reasons for being attracted to some portraits rather than others. In the next stage the number of selected portraits has to be reduced to the sixty that will hang in the exhibition, and here judges articulate their feelings and opinions, sometimes passionately and certainly emphatically, about what really works for each of them. In the final stage the prize-winning portraits are picked. This is agonising as so many deserve prizes and only four can be short-listed and one chosen for the Godfrey Argent Award.

Even where the judges differ greatly in their opinions, I am keen that they should understand and respect each others' judgements. That range of viewpoint complements the extraordinary diversity of what is submitted: portraits taken by an increasingly international group of photographers. The use of colour, black and white, analogue or digital technologies, as well as scale, lighting and technique, all play their part in making a great portrait. Finally, the best photographic portraits translate a living person across time and place, giving the illusion that we, the viewers, can now see and meet them in the Gallery. It is a great art.

I want to acknowledge and thank all the many talented photographers from around the world who submitted a record 6,900 images to the 2007 Photographic Portrait Prize. Many congratulations go to this year's winners: Jonathan Torgovnik, Julieta Sans, Michelle Sank, David Stewart and Ivor Prickett, winner of the Godfrey Argent Award. This year this special award is given to a portrait photographer aged twenty-five or under. It represents the Gallery's continuing interest in encouraging younger photographers of talent to submit their work and to be judged alongside their peers. We are very grateful to the estate of Godfrey Argent for enabling us to include it this year.

I should like to thank my fellow judges: Cheryl Newman, Terence Pepper, Sheila Rock and Sue Steward. They worked extraordinarily hard for two long days and were passionate, forthright and determined in their choices. My thanks also go to Pim Baxter, Claudia Bloch, Catherine Bromley, Naomi Conway, Denise Elitson, Neil Evans, Clare Freestone, Celia Joicey, Ruth Müller-Wirth, Jonathan Rowbotham, Sarah Tinsley and especially Sue Thompson, as well as other National Portrait Gallery staff, the designers NB: Studio and the interviewer Richard McClure, for all their hard work on the exhibition and the catalogue. I am also grateful to the white wall company for their contribution to the administration and judging process.

Sandy Nairne, Director,
National Portrait Gallery

Judging the Competition

Editing photographs is a magical process. The judgment – 'possible', 'no' or 'the one' – can happen in a split second, as eyes skim and survey, and brain centres incorporate personal aesthetics and political or social values. We five jurors made such decisions thousands of times during this hunt for winners, and intense discussion wasn't often possible when working at this scale, but when 'the one' passed by, my reaction was to catch breath and sit upright in my chair.

Interestingly, after seeing the short-listed images once, twice or three times, sometimes the original passion would evaporate and a photograph's former appeal would seem baffling. Yet the selected sixty, including five winners, stay with me still: a sign that the magic was at work and we chose well. All five of us, with personal differences and various photographic backgrounds, recognized *Joseline Ingabire with her daughter Leah Batamuliza, Rwanda* by Jonathan Torgovnik, as possessing special qualities (p.7). Three dark-skinned women are presented against the subdued backdrop of the sandy earth and their mud-walled house, staring impassively at the camera. The woman with her arms round the girl emits a calm which contrasts with the cacophony of patterns on her robes. For a split second, the scene's photogenicity deceived me into wondering, another travel photograph? But there was something too quiet here, which gradually appeared as sadness. The word 'Rwanda' in the title conjured old news reports about children conceived during the Rwanda war after rape by enemy soldiers. Even if we had never known the location or the cruel secret, I am sure that this image would have remained in the selection: its stirring narrative, matching a reality for other women worldwide, played a key part in its attraction.

Few other submissions carried such layers of meaning and relevance in today's global turbulence. *Slavika feeds her baby son Nikola while her husband Nebojsa sleeps* by Ivor Prickett (p.15) also possesses a deceptive tranquillity and conceals an insecure past behind a similarly classic scenario. Illuminated delicately from the left of the frame, this image has a medieval quality with biblical overtones evoked by the composition of the family trio. The suggestion is exile, maybe refugee status (and war), and, here again, the title adds resonance to a situation shared by the millions living in tents, containers or hostels.

In the real world, we are at war. But, surprisingly, the only explicit reference to this is the painterly scene set in a US army bunker in Afghanistan, where a camouflaged soldier sits quietly smoking in her tent against a backdrop of almost too perfectly toned sand, sandbags and canvas (p.45). Its perfection suggests a film set – or a set-up – the soldier playing a reality game.

An overwhelming number of the images carry our enduring fascination with the beauty and self-awareness of young women as they hover on the blurred borders between childhood and adulthood. Those contradictory pulls make for revealing, sometimes disturbing portraits. The self-harming girl *Janine* by Michelle Sank defiantly exposes the slashed scars up her arm – and her vulnerability (p.11); the girl in the 'Drop Dead' T-shirt in *Alice & Fish* by David Stewart holds a dead fish on a stick (p.13). Both collude with the photographer in their staginess. Yet the pervasive lack of energy and expressiveness usually associated with this strand of portraiture contradicts the ebullience and uninhibited loudness of that generation. Fortunately, there are many sweet, lyrical, sensual-to-erotic and intriguing exceptions.

The naked girl posing in a garage close to a set of golf clubs and a pair of neatly positioned mules, *Hiromi Yamaguchi Migas* by Richard Boll (p.67), possesses great freshness and raises all kinds of narrative alternatives. Another of my favourites, *Lucila, a.m.* by Julieta Sans, features a young woman sitting cross-legged in her dressing gown on the floor by a window (p.9). Oblivious to the camera, she could be the object of a fond reflective study but for the small visible patch of underwear which lends a provocative frisson – and the question, does she know what we know?

This emphasis on youth tips the balance away from last year's selection which included a marvellously classic portrait of the legendary icons of British photography, Grace Robertson and Thurston Hopkins. Even this year's flock of baby pictures lacks the sharpness, near-surreality and erotic playfulness seen in 2006, or the subverted sentimentality of Tom Craig's young woman kissing her baby's head in a field. I found it most surprising that the majority of submissions took a literal approach to their subject. Safeness overwhelms, and also a reliance on influences from previous years' themes and winners and recent blockbuster exhibitions; the lyrical shot of a girl skating in Beijing, *Ice Rink* by Charlie Crane (above right and p.66), with mist rising off the ice, is a perfect evocation of the work of Andreas Gursky. We were bemused by certain recurrences in the original entries: red-headed children followed a now established Photographic Portrait Prize tradition, and retro displays of scars and bruises recalled *The Face's* controversial trendsetters in the late 1980s. Several examples, however, showed a new trend for displaying heart-transplant zip-scars.

Of the refreshingly different submissions, a Cartier Bresson 'frozen moment' at Holborn viaduct, *Beth* by Frederic Huska (below and p.27), involves a young woman waiting in front of a giant reproduction of the original construction; the men hew at rocks as the woman waits anxiously, her scarf blowing. Interweaving several stories, it introduces a change of scale from the many domestic interiors (and many fascinating, cluttered rooms).

One of the challenges and pleasures of selecting this group show is trying to discover unifying themes and new directions, ideas that sum up a time or a zeitgeist while also exploring new ways to express our fast-changing world. The overwhelming sensation here was of talented young photographers preferring the security of working within established styles. Maybe next year will be a more radical appraisal of the times?

Sue Steward, writer, broadcaster, photography critic for the *Evening Standard* and Arts Correspondent for British Airways Highlife radio.

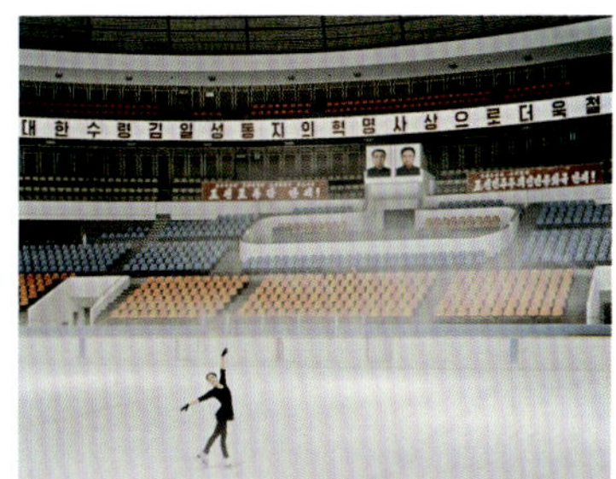

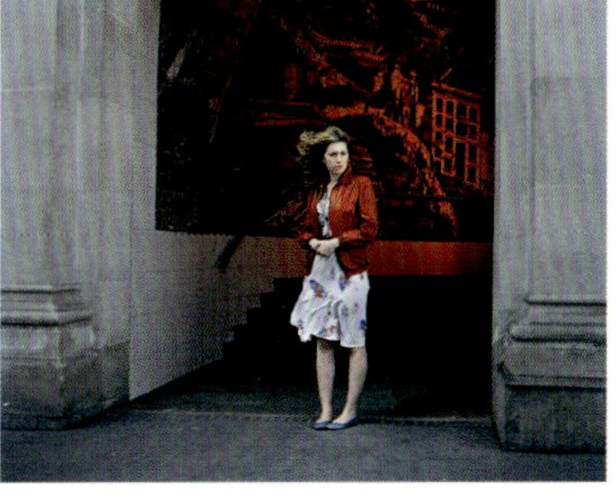

The Prizes

Photographic Portrait Prize

The Photographic Portrait Prize is open to photographers from around the world aged eighteen or over.

The first prize winner is Jonathan Torgovnik, who receives £12,000.

The second prize winner is Julieta Sans, who receives £3,000.

The third prize winner is Michelle Sank, who receives £2,000.

The fourth prize winner is David Stewart, who receives £1,000.

The Godfrey Argent Award

The Godfrey Argent Award is given this year to the best entry taken by a photographer aged twenty-five or under.

The winner is Ivor Prickett, who receives £2,500.

If you would like to join the mailing list to receive an entry form for next year's Photographic Portrait Prize, please send your full contact details to:

Photographic Portrait Prize 2008
Marketing Department
National Portrait Gallery
St Martin's Place
London WC2H 0HE
photoprize@npg.org.uk

The Judges

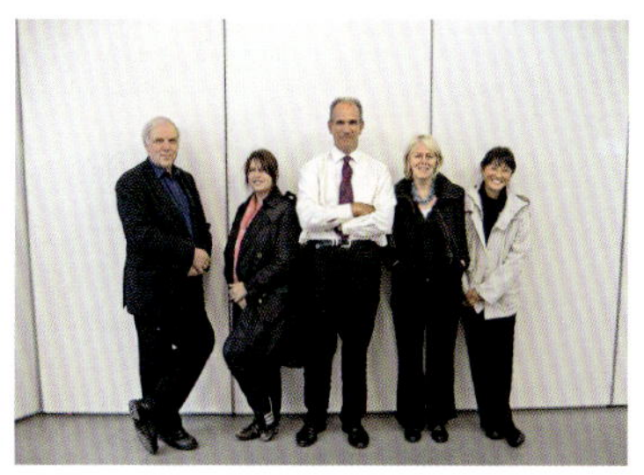

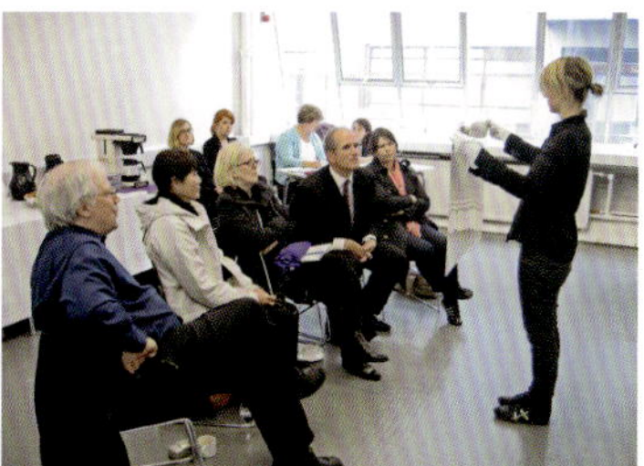

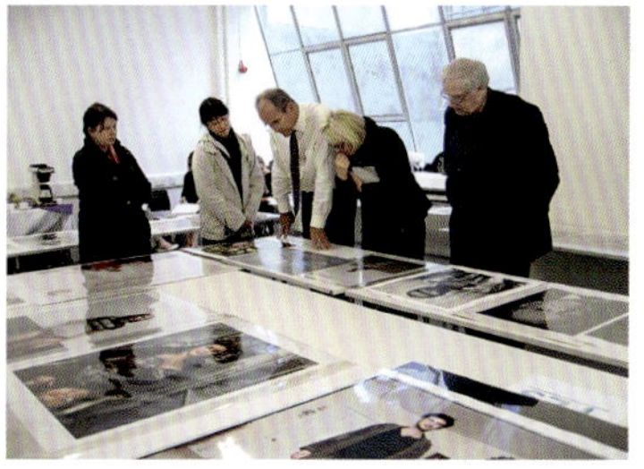

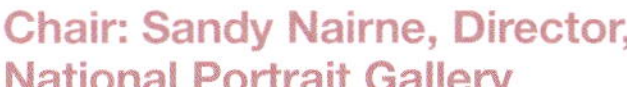

Chair: Sandy Nairne, Director, National Portrait Gallery

2007 was an exceptional year in terms of both the quantity and quality of the submissions. Viewing the work of more than 2,700 photographers and 6,900 images was incredibly exciting, as the whole world seemed to be present. Without knowing the identity of the photographer, we scrutinized each image to try and find that special quality which makes a great portrait stand out. As always, there were more good portraits than prizes to go round, and I would like to pay tribute to so many diverse talents offering new ideas about contemporary portraiture.

Cheryl Newman, Comissioning Photography Editor, *Saturday Telegraph Magazine*

Being asked to judge the Portrait Prize was a real honour and I was excited to meet the challenge. I edit photographic portraits and photo-stories for a living, so I'm used to making fast but considered judgements about the narrative worth, significance and beauty of photos. The inclusion of pictures in the magazine I work on is negotiated from both a text and a layout perspective: I work closely with both the art director and the editor.

Judging a portrait prize is a different kind of battlefield. I had to find common ground with four other photo geeks, all experts in their different walks of the picture world and armed with different preferences, tastes and whims. One thing we did all share was an astonishment at the diversity and range of the work, and surprise at the incredible volume of amateur images, for the most part babies and kittens.

Although we looked at over 6,000 images, for me the treasures were easy to spot, especially as many photographers took a multiple-image approach adding context and meaning to their work. Some pictures were the subject of fierce debate, particularly where the panel was split between two images, while others such as the sensitive interior by Ivor Prickett or the beauty and form of Jonathan Torgovnik's Rwanda portraits were decisions made unanimously and almost instantly.

Awards unearth and nourish talent and this prize is an integral part of the ever-changing, pulsing, growing, mutating creature that is the photography world.

Terence Pepper, Curator of Photographs, National Portrait Gallery

Judging the annual Photographic Portrait Prize is always a bittersweet experience. As Charles Dickens wrote: 'It was the best of times, it was the worst of times.' Having the wonderful opportunity of looking at almost 7,000 prints, which were some of the most inventive, insightful, amusing, strange, poignant, sad or just plain beautiful portraits from all over the world, was a rare privilege. It is one of the best experiences for any photographic curator. But it was 'the worst of times' having to reduce them to only sixty finalists for the show and just hoping that all those unsuccessful entrants would not be discouraged and would keep producing interesting work.

Sheila Rock, photographer

The judging process has been an extraordinary experience. It is a great privilege to see wonderful images and thousands of photographs that touch on many universal social themes. The Photographic Portrait Prize is a reflection of our constantly changing view of people in our society and also forms a part of the great tradition of portraiture that runs through history. It was very stimulating to choose from the enormous range of images by photographers from all around the world covering so many aspects of different societies today. The result has been the selection of distinguished images that capture the changing moods of our times.

Sue Steward, writer and broadcaster

Even the most hardened photo-editors practised in speedy viewing and instant decision-making would quiver at the prospect of sampling over 6,900 portraits in two days. But the well-practised system, involving a slow flash-past of prints by handlers wearing white gloves, made it relatively painless – and by the end of day two, we had survived the complex mental processes that reduced us to silent concentration, and the winners lay on trestle tables like jewels. While we all regretted the absence of one or two favourites that we hadn't been able to coerce the others to agree on, we had arrived at remarkably harmonious collective decisions – a model of democracy.

The process raised ebbs and flows of excitement, eye-rolling amusement and dismay, and wonderful surprises. The deluge of family-album imagery was dominated by breast-feeding women, cute babies and pets, but few rose above the mundane and sentimental. I anticipated the profusion of pre-teens and young teenagers with listless expressions, and there they were. Their popularity reflects an enduring strand within portrait photography, but I missed seeing the dignified beauty at the other end of the age spectrum. There were many contributions from and in foreign countries, whose seductively photogenic faces, costumes and settings distracted from character or context. Then the overall winner appeared quietly and we nodded in unison, because this image implies something of the woman's story while being a stunning study in colour and composition. This intense experience left a kaleidoscope of fragmented images and colours hijacking my vision for days.

First Prize Winner Jonathan Torgovnik

Born in 1969 in Tel Aviv, Jonathan Torgovnik began his career as a combat photographer in the Israeli army, documenting military activity in Gaza and the West Bank. By the age of eighteen, his images were already being syndicated to the world press. 'The army was my school of photography,' says Torgovnik. 'I was sent into the field without any instruction and ordered to take pictures. They just told me to go out there and shoot, but instead of a gun, I had a camera.'

He moved to New York in his early twenties, where he graduated from the School of Visual Arts. He has since received numerous awards for his portraiture and documentary news features, which have appeared in publications such as *Vanity Fair*, the *Sunday Times Magazine* and most recently *Newsweek*, which he joined as a contract photographer in 2005.

It was while covering a story on the HIV epidemic in Africa for *Newsweek* that Torgovnik first met Tutsi women who had been victims of sexual violence during the 1994 genocide in Rwanda. According to humanitarian groups, an estimated 20,000 children in Rwanda were born from rape. 'It was the most horrific thing I'd ever heard,' says Torgovnik. 'The trauma these women went through was beyond anything I could imagine.'

Torgovnik has returned to the country twice, photographing around thirty women and their children for his photo series *Intended Consequences: Mothers of Genocide, Children of Rape*, which includes his winning entry in the Photographic Portrait Prize, *Joseline Ingabire with her daughter Leah Batamuliza, Rwanda*.

'When the genocide started, Joseline was married and two months pregnant. The militia came to her village and brutally killed her husband in front of her. Immediately after that she was raped.' Joseline was raped continually throughout her pregnancy, even at nine months, and again after she gave birth to her husband's daughter, who is pictured in the background of the portrait. Following countless sexual assaults, Joseline became pregnant again, eventually giving birth to Leah. 'Joseline has two daughters who are less than one year apart,' says Torgovnik. 'One is born from love, the other is born from rape. Neither girl is yet aware of the situation.'

Although the 38-year-old photographer has covered many harrowing stories during his career, including features on Meth addicts in the US and victims of cholera in Bangladesh, he admits he has been moved to tears by his Rwandan work. He shot the series with a Hasselblad 6x6 square format, but there were occasions when Torgovnik was too distressed to work. 'One woman's story was so sad that I couldn't take any pictures. I was so numb I had to come back the next day. Many of the women have HIV from the rape and are also living in extreme poverty. Emotionally, it has affected me very deeply, so much so that I am trying to give something back.'

To this end, Torgovnik has set up a foundation to raise funds to pay for the children to have a secondary education, which costs $150 per year (www.foundationrwanda.org). 'The women have very complex relationships with their children, but they all want to give them an education, so this is where I hope to be some help. This project is very personal for me – it has become a kind of mission. I am not interested in being the detached photographer. In this case, I am very attached.'

Interviewed by Richard McClure

Jonathan Torgovnik

Joseline Ingabire with her daughter Leah Batamuliza, Rwanda
from the series
Intended Consequences: Mothers of Genocide, Children of Rape
September 2006

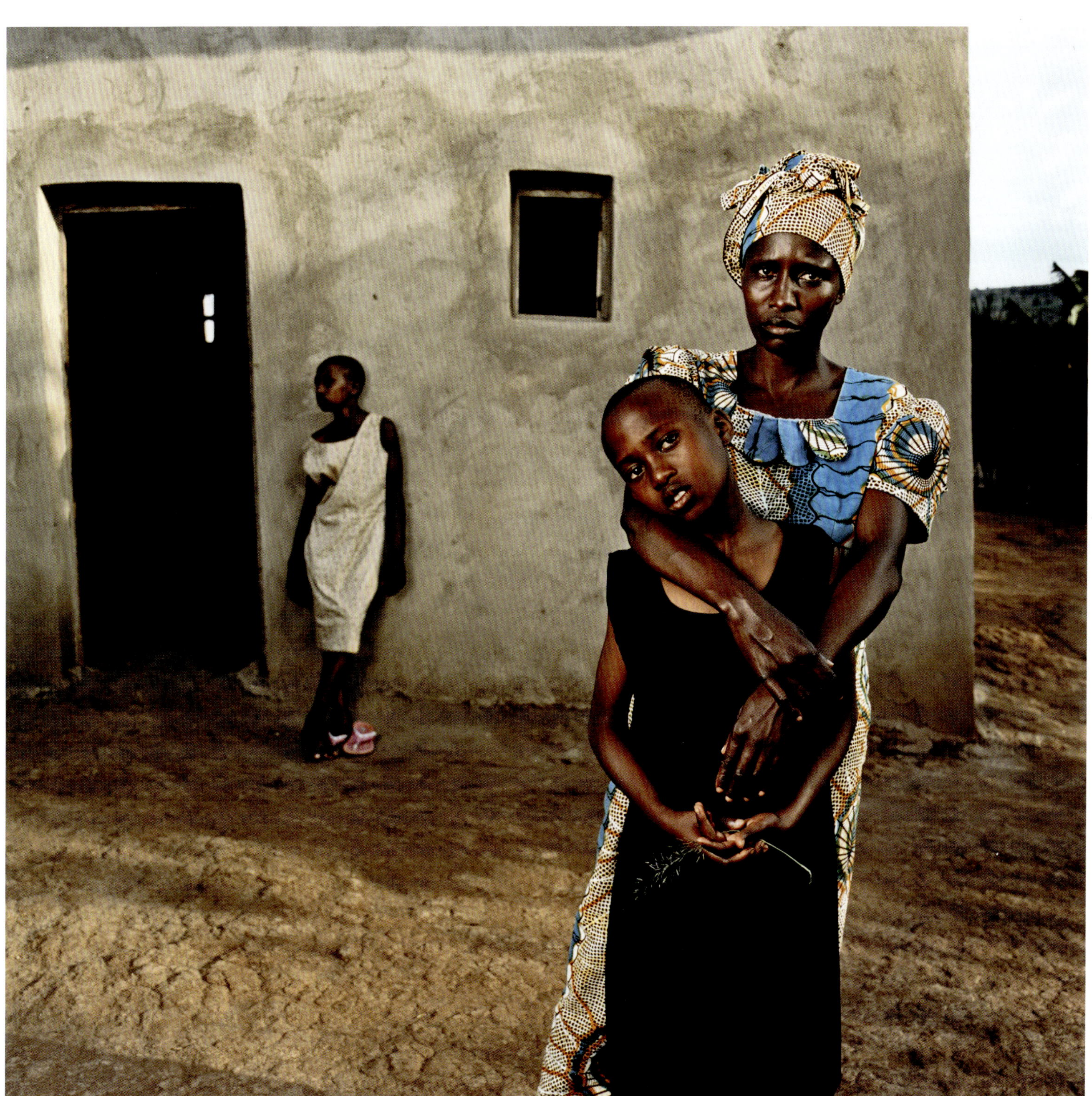

Second Prize Winner Julieta Sans

A return visit to her native Argentina allowed Julieta Sans the opportunity to continue work on a long-term photographic project in which she records friends and acquaintances in the quiet intimacy of their everyday rituals. Her entry, *Lucila, a.m.*, portrays a close friend at home in Buenos Aires as she prepares for the day ahead. 'That morning I woke up and went to see Lucila in her room, where she was eating breakfast and epilating her legs,' says Sans. 'The photo shoot was very improvised. I intervened very little in the scene, limiting myself to observing her gestures and suggesting subtle changes. The way in which I photograph is very instinctive. I do it without asking myself many questions.'

Shot with a Rolleiflex 6x6, with a white reflector to bounce natural light back onto Lucila, the portrait captures the sitter at a crossroads in her life as she debates whether to move out of the family nest. 'Most middle-class people in Buenos Aires have a family structure to rely on and it's often easier to live in the comfort of your parents' home than start an independent life,' explains Sans. 'Lucila was faced with the choice of whether to take the plunge into adulthood by getting her own place and a job, or stay with her parents and linger in a sort of prolonged adolescence. Despite the fact that she is evidently a grown woman, there are details in the portrait, such as her pose, her haircut and the badly painted toenails, that give away this reluctance to grow up.'

Now aged twenty-eight, Sans made her own bid for independence in 2003 when she left home and settled in London, gaining a Postgraduate Certificate in Photography from Central Saint Martins in 2005. Her interest in the medium had developed as a teenager when she started using her mother's old Pentax during a family holiday in Brazil. 'In the beginning I used to photograph myself and my sister; I did many abstract portraits and nudes and loved Francesca Woodman and Sarah Moon.'

Currently completing a 'playful and loving' portfolio of people posing as their favourite literary characters, Sans combines personal projects with freelance research work in commercials, assisting directors in their pitches and sourcing visual and film references to illustrate their ideas. 'My plan is to keep working in research as well as doing editorial and documentary assignments,' she says. 'I am not really interested in any genre other than portraiture. It is mainly people that I am drawn to, and the desire to understand and get close to them. Perhaps that is because I am quite shy and I prefer to step back and observe rather than be at the centre of things. As a photographer, I am interested in the moment where people let their guard down and show themselves in their vulnerability.'

Interviewed by Richard McClure

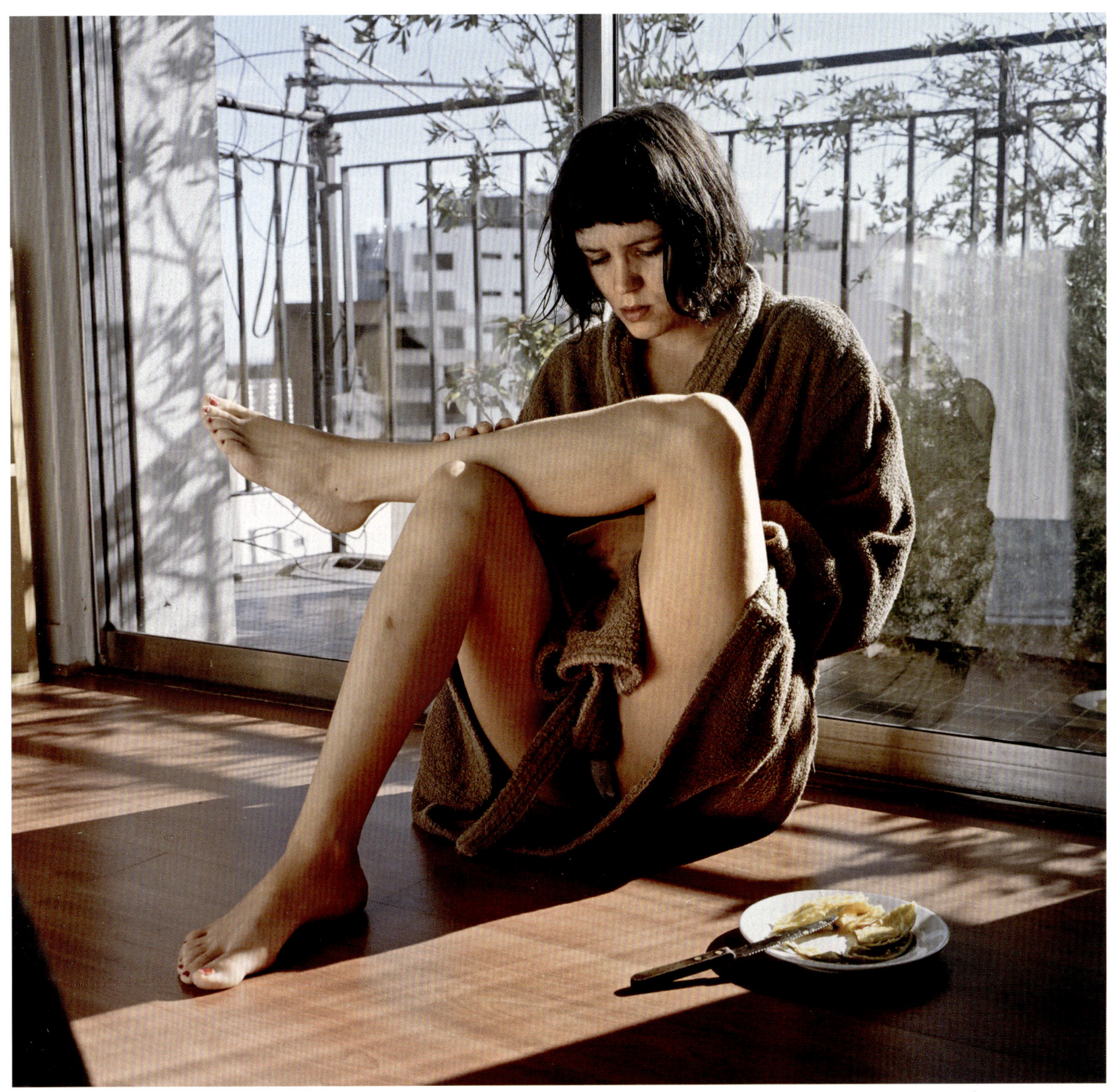

Third Prize Winner Michelle Sank

Although Michelle Sank has lived in the UK for the past twenty years, the Exeter-based photographer believes her portraits of teenagers are deeply rooted in her South African upbringing. Born in Cape Town to Russian immigrants, she graduated with a fine art degree before switching to camera work, encouraged by David Goldblatt, one of the country's most celebrated photographers. Her promising career was interrupted, however, by South Africa's worsening political crisis, and in 1978 Sank left for a new life in Europe.

'Things were very, very bad. I was viewing violence and extreme brutality on a daily basis,' recalls Sank. 'I also experienced a lot of anti-Semitism and I felt terribly isolated. There were a lot of kids who had no future because of the huge injustice of the apartheid regime. That somehow feeds into my work. My portraits have never made political statements, but I have always been drawn to people on the edge of society.'

Financial hardship forced Sank to take a publishing job in Greece before she moved to England in 1987, eventually reigniting her passion for photography in 1999 with an MA at the University of Leicester, where she developed her signature style of 'compassionate' portraiture set against open skies. 'I need to work outdoors. Light and space are very important to me – that also comes from Africa. Cloud formations are very prevalent in my work; they often have an emotional or spiritual significance.'

Sank's entry, *Janine from Reality Crossings,* is taken from the photo series *Reality Crossings, Germany*, which documents a day centre for troubled teens in Mannheim, Germany. 'I knew when I photographed Janine that something powerful was happening. At first sight, she seems very self-assured and empowered – only then is your eye drawn to the scars and scratches on her arm. Her self-harming signals a cry for help, and also shows the complexity of adolescence. There was a real sadness about some of the kids at the centre. Many were dealing with a lack of family or parents who take no interest in them.'

Sank's preoccupation with youth culture has resulted in a number of gallery residencies throughout the UK and Europe, including projects concerning teenage mothers and juvenile ex-offenders. In 2004, Cardiff's Ffotogallery commissioned a series of portraits of young carers, followed in 2005 by *Teenage Belfast*, an exhibition at Belfast Exposed Photography, in which Sank sought to portray her young subjects as 'positive symbols of a new and developing society'. Images from these series were included in her first book, *Becoming*, published in 2006.

Away from photography, Sank also works in the youth justice system as a mentor to disaffected adolescents in Devon. 'I have great empathy with these kids – it's important to me that my photographs allow them their dignity and humanity. My portraits have always had an element of social enlightenment. I don't tune into negativity. When I work with kids who have problems, I don't see the problem, I see only the person.'

Interviewed by Richard McClure

Michelle Sank

Janine from Reality Crossings *from the series* Reality Crossings, Germany
July 2007

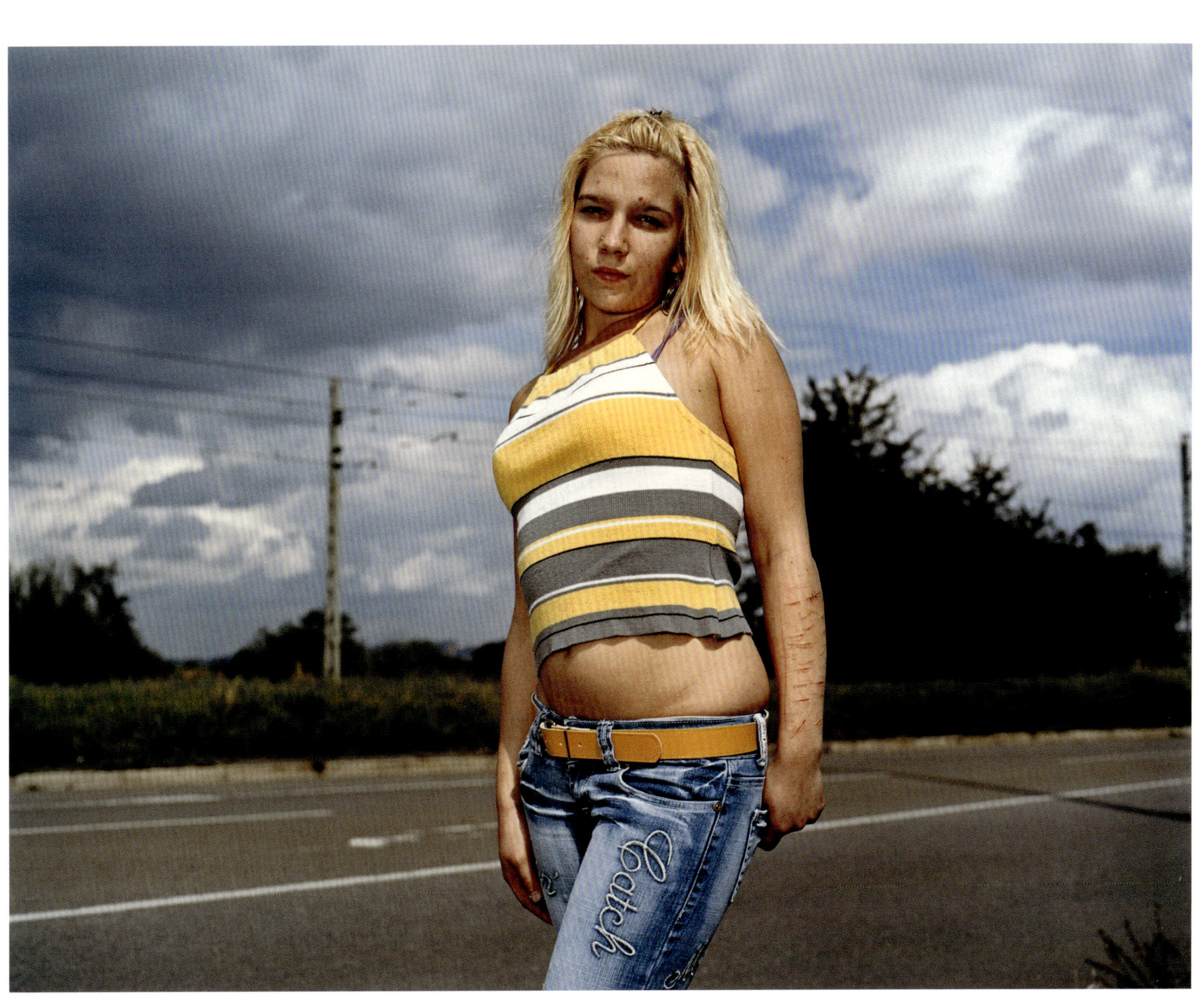

Fourth Prize Winner David Stewart

Commercial photographer David Stewart is no stranger to the Photographic Portrait Prize, having exhibited several times in previous years, most recently in 2006 with an image of his elderly father. His entry this year, *Alice & Fish*, features another family member, his 14-year-old daughter, who was photographed among the seagrass beds of Morecambe Bay during a visit to Stewart's home town of Lancaster. Both portraits are taken from *Relations*, a light-hearted series that Stewart has been working on for three years. 'The series isn't about family relations as such; rather it is loosely based on visual connections between people, places and animals,' he explains.

Looking to restore the 'mystery that is missing from digital photography', he shot his portrait of Alice in large format with an old-style, wooden, drop-baseboard, 10x8 camera. 'At the time, Alice was full of teenage attitude and going through an "emo" phase,' says Stewart. 'She and her friends were always so miserable that I thought it would be fun to pose her with an equally gloomy looking fish. It seemed a nice fit. Humour is a big part of my work – I like gently poking fun at people.'

Stewart's own teenage years were spent photographing punk bands, including The Clash and The Ramones, as they performed at local venues. 'The photographs were purely for my own pleasure, and looking back, they were pretty awful pictures. But I enjoyed it so much that my plans to be a civil engineer quickly went out of the window.'

After studying photography at Blackpool and The Fylde College, Stewart moved to London in 1981, assisting for three years before setting up his own studio. He has since become one of the UK's most sought-after advertising photographers, producing campaigns for the likes of Coca-Cola, American Express, Vodafone, Toyota and MasterCard.

Besides his commercial work, Stewart's portraits have featured in two publications. His first collection, *Cabbage*, a surrealistic tribute to the much maligned vegetable, was accompanied by a short film that was nominated for a BAFTA in 1995. *Fogeys*, published in 2001, comprised 'kitsch, cartoon-like photographs of people growing old disgracefully', whether zooming downhill on a go-kart or lounging in a coffin-shaped paddling pool. Exhibited at the ICA, London, *Fogeys* also won a silver award at the Art Directors Club of New York.

'My personal projects used to be as staged and as manipulated as my ads. For *Fogeys*, I used a lot of people from model agencies and big visual puns,' says Stewart. 'But my exhibition work is changing: humour is no longer the dominant element and the set-up is usually much more hidden. The portrait of Alice is more observational and character-based. Everything is less blatant, less obvious. I want people to look deeper into the photograph in order to discover the detail and the subtleties.'

Interviewed by Richard McClure

David Stewart

Alice & Fish
from the series
Relations
October 2006

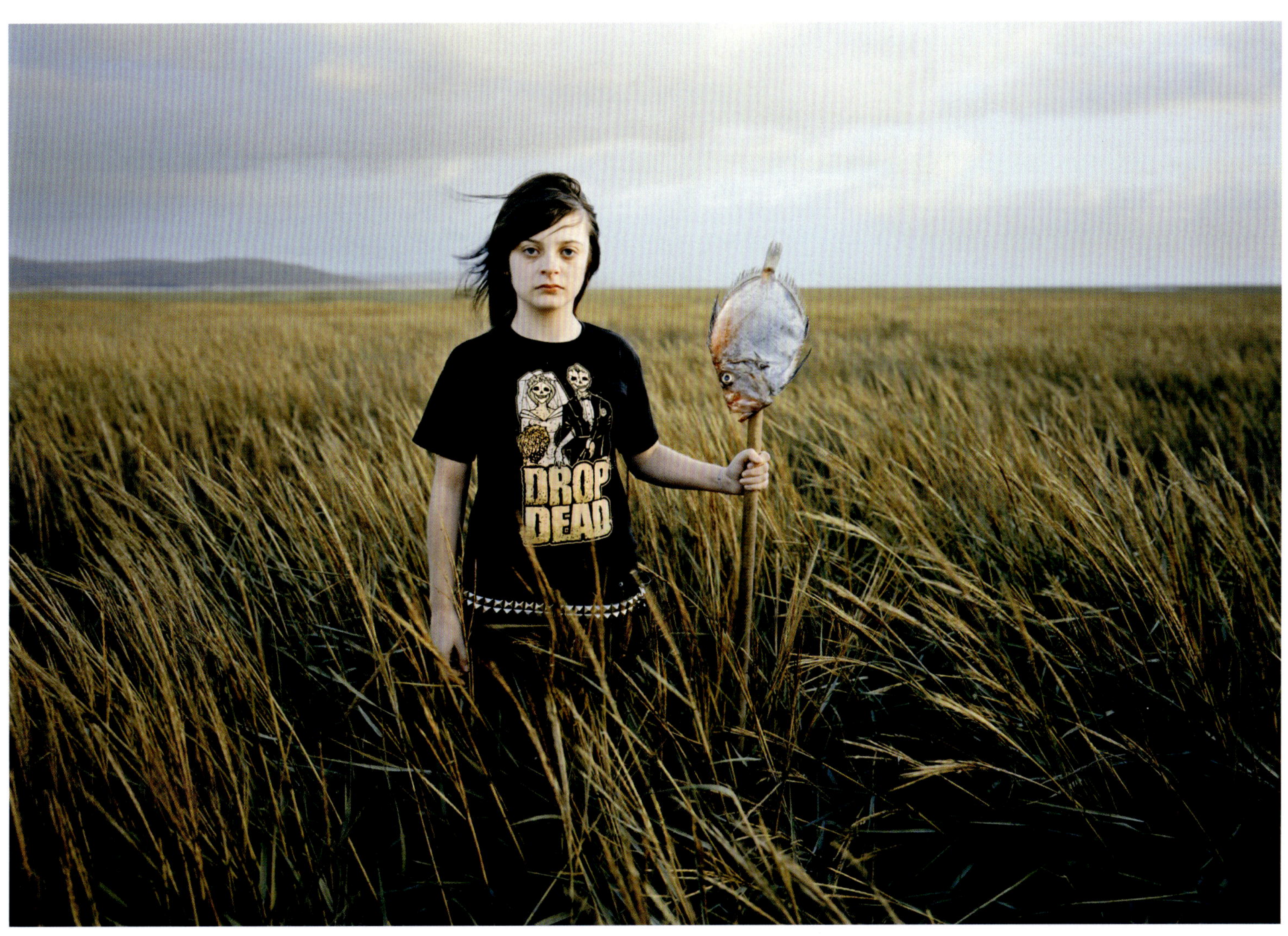

The Godfrey Argent Award Winner Ivor Prickett

Winner of the Godfrey Argent Award for the best portrait taken by a photographer aged twenty-five or under, Ivor Prickett studied documentary photography at the University of Wales, Newport. Graduating with First Class Honours in 2006, he is now based in London, working as a freelance photographer and focusing on humanitarian issues in the former Yugoslavia.

Shortly after finishing his degree, Prickett spent a month living with several Serbian families who had returned to Croatia after being displaced from their homes during the Balkans conflict. In 1995, the Croatian army launched the notorious military offensive Operation Storm, ruthlessly 'cleansing' Serbs from their enclave in the Criena, destroying thousands of homes and purging the region of its non-Croat population.

Taken from Prickett's photo essay *The Quiet After the Storm*, his winning entry, *Slavica feeds her baby son Nikola while her husband Nebojsa sleeps*, depicts Serbian factory worker Nebojsa Eremic following his return to Croatia with his wife Slavica and their 10-month-old baby, Nikola.

'Nebojsa was among 200,000 Serbs displaced by Operation Storm, and he fled with his parents to Serbia,' explains Prickett. 'He came back to Croatia two years later, but even today life is very hard for the returnees, who face huge problems reintegrating. At the time the picture was taken, Nebojsa was unemployed and the family was living in a tiny cottage with little money. In some ways, however, it is a beautiful vignette. Slavica is an incredibly elegant, serene figure and I think the portrait captures the family's stasis, a sense of their lives being on hold.'

Prickett shot the portrait in medium format with a Bronica SQ-Ai, a change from the 35mm he had used previously to photograph the displacement of Roma gypsies from their homes in Kosovo, a project for which he won the Tom Webster Award in 2005. 'Medium format is about slowing down, thinking more about the context of the picture,' he explains. 'I switched from 35mm because I am not interested in roaming around, doing "immediate" photography. I don't want to steal a picture without knowing anything about the person's situation.'

In August 2007, the Irish-born photographer won the BJP/Nikon Endframe Award for his Croatian portfolio. He is now using the bursary to continue his work in the Balkans while also taking on editorial commissions, including a recent assignment photographing Madagascan gold mines for the *Daily Telegraph*. With three major awards to his name at the age of twenty-four, Prickett says he is 'much more positive' about pursuing a career in photojournalism. 'It's been hard for me to survive because I don't do commercial work of any sort,' he says. 'But the recognition has really given me the confidence to continue what I love doing.'

Interviewed by Richard McClure

Ivor Prickett

Slavica feeds her baby son Nikola while her husband Nebojsa sleeps *from the series* The Quiet After the Storm July 2006

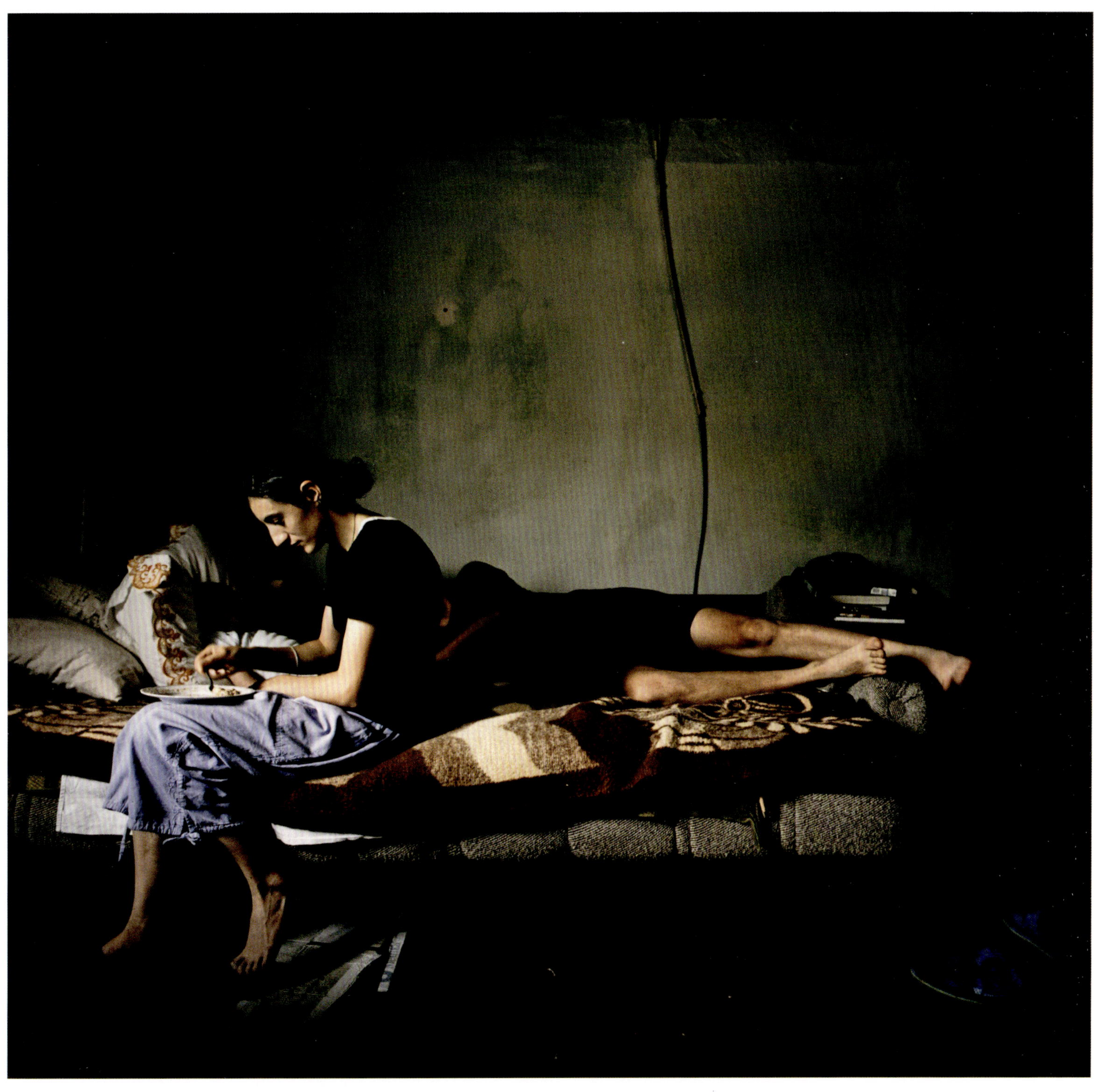

Exhibitors

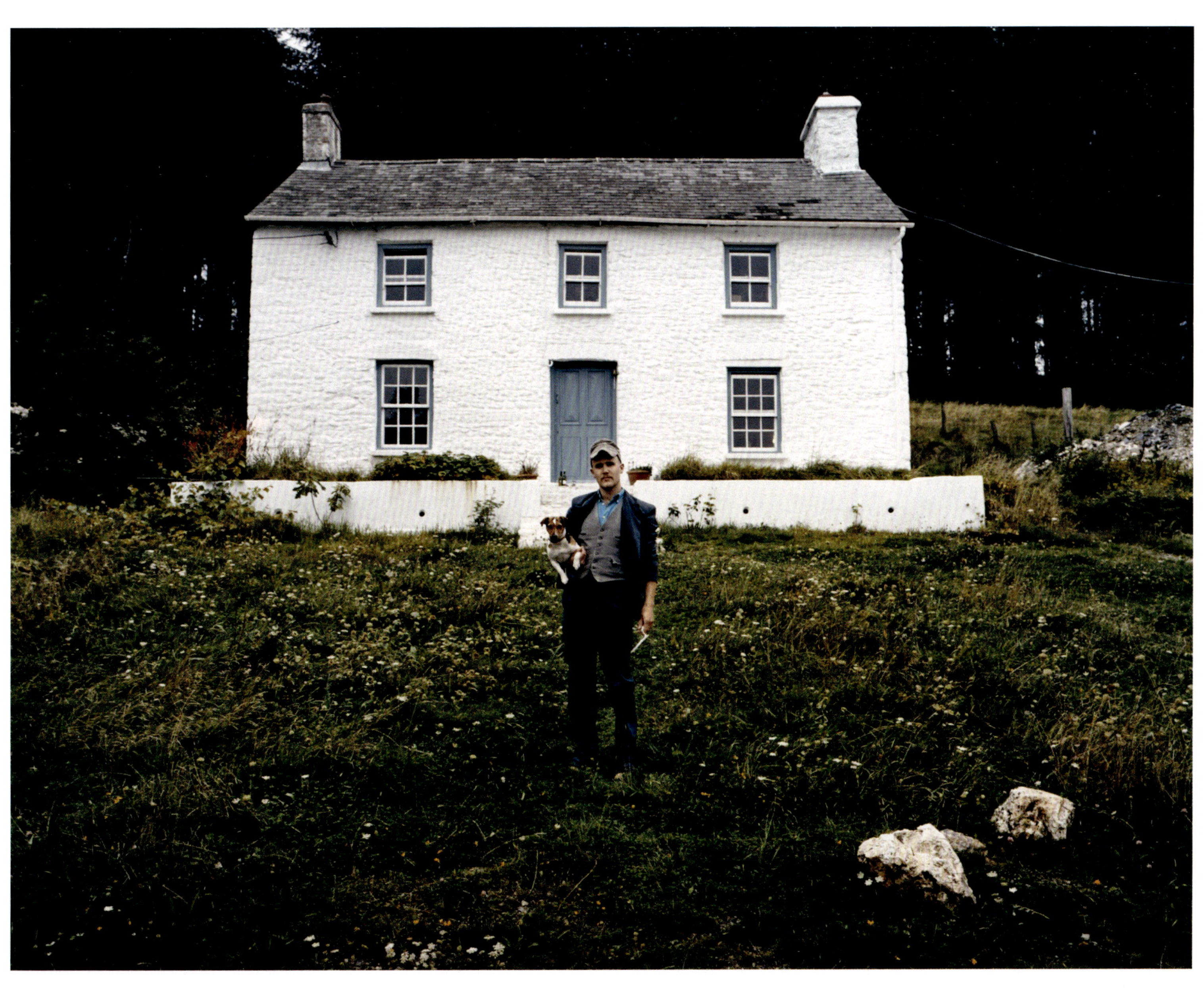

Venetia Dearden

Untitled
from the series
21st-Century Living
September 2006

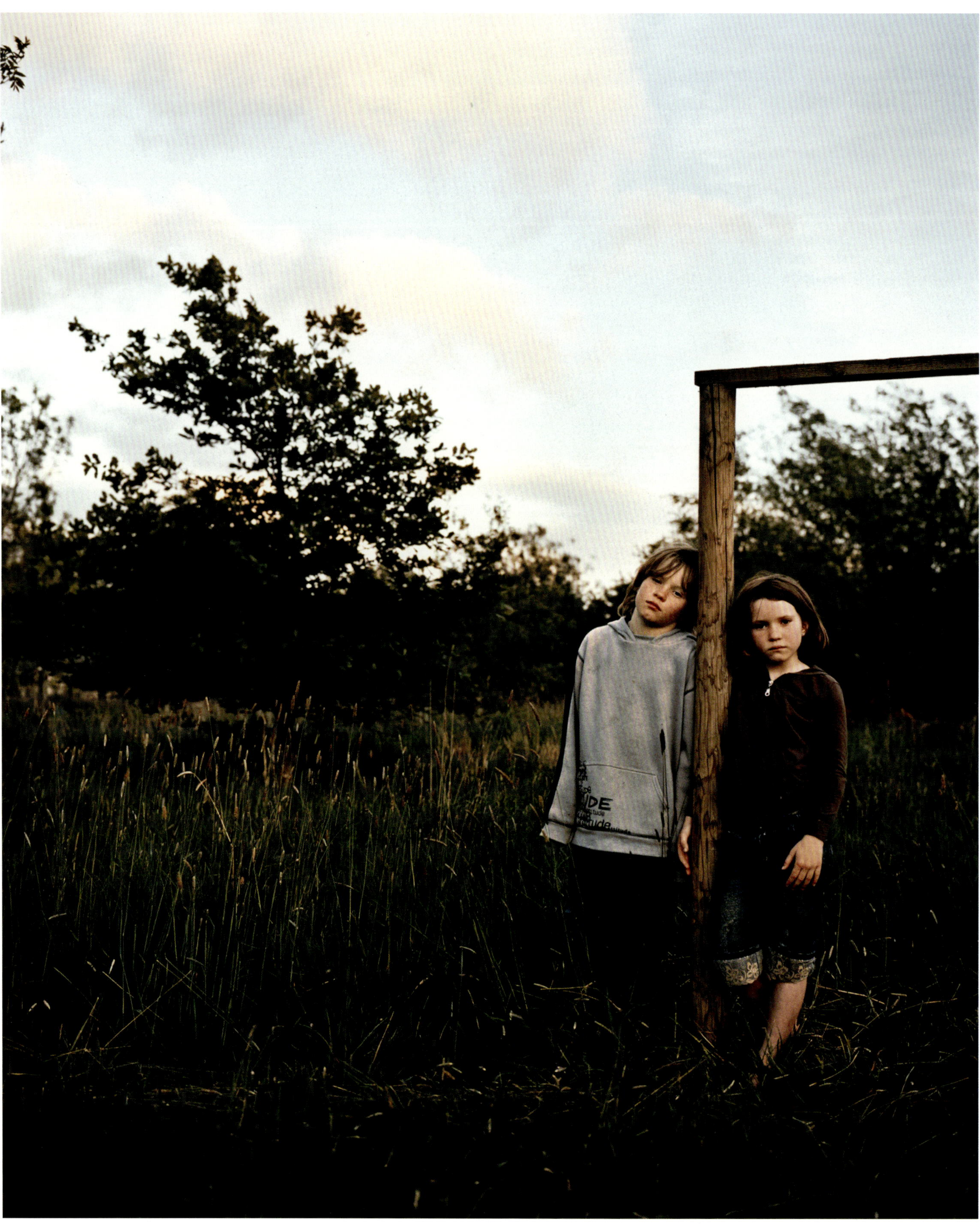

Corrina Adams

Holly
from the series
Travellers
May 2007

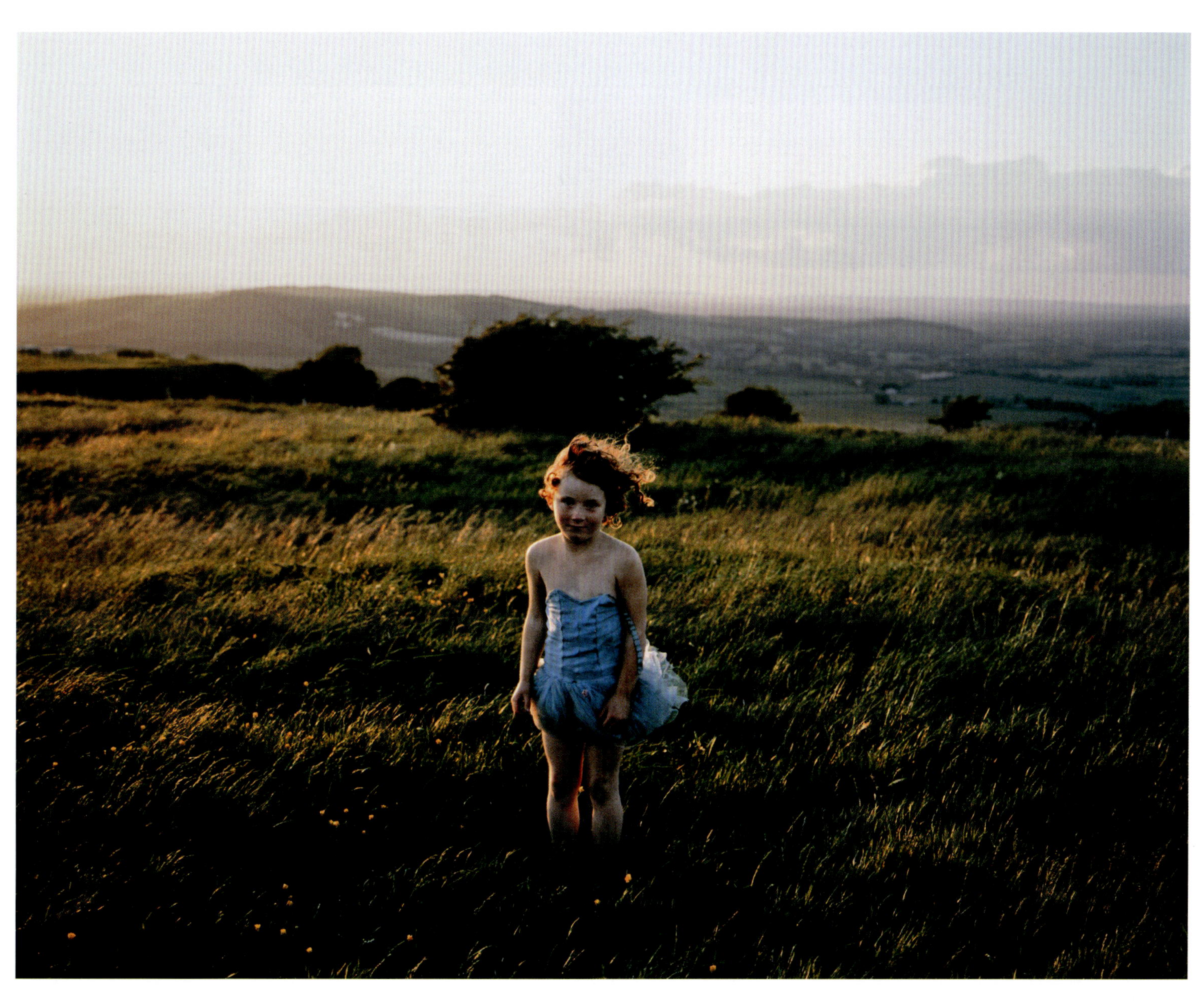

Haris Artemis

Two Who Care
from the series
Who Cares
May 2007

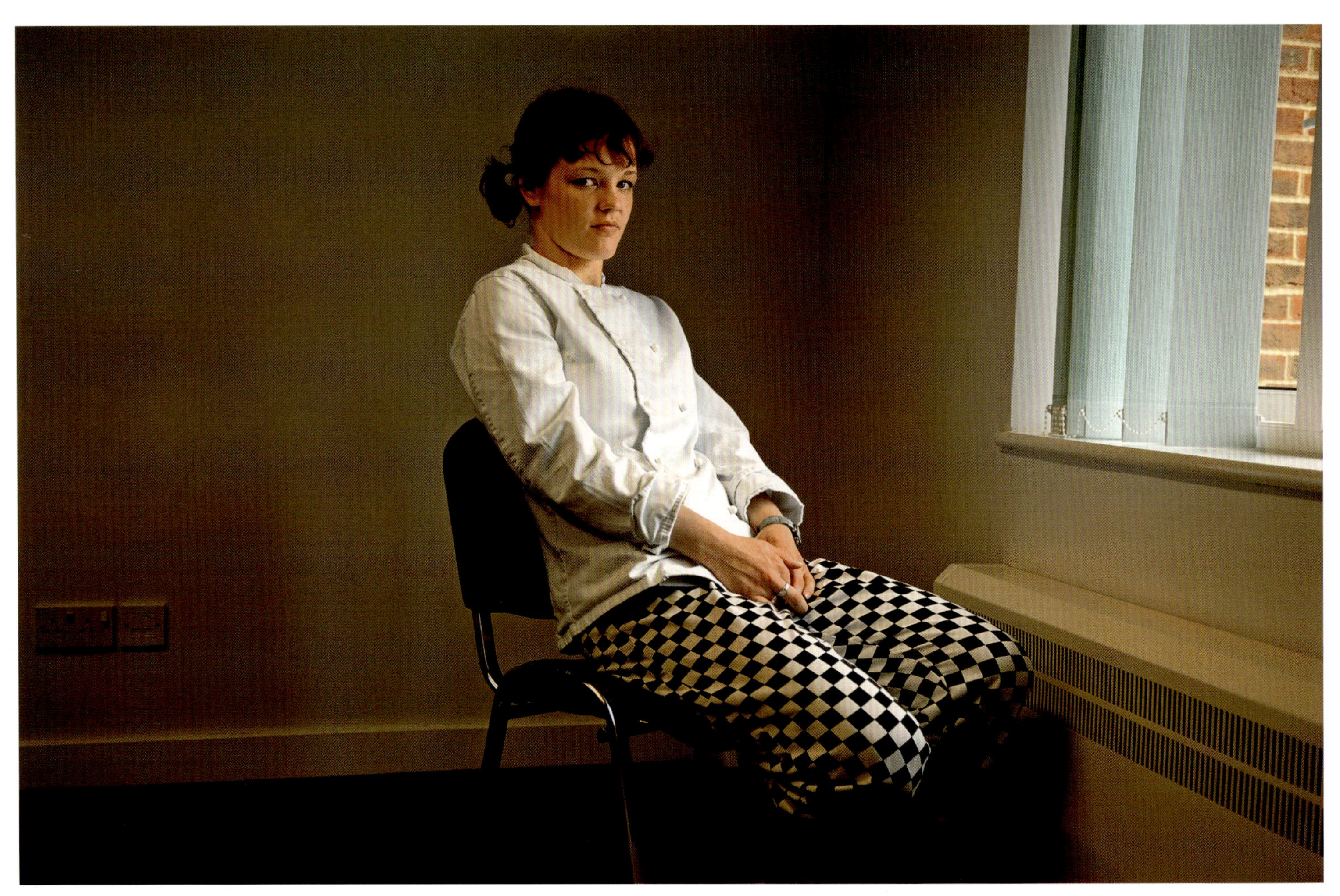

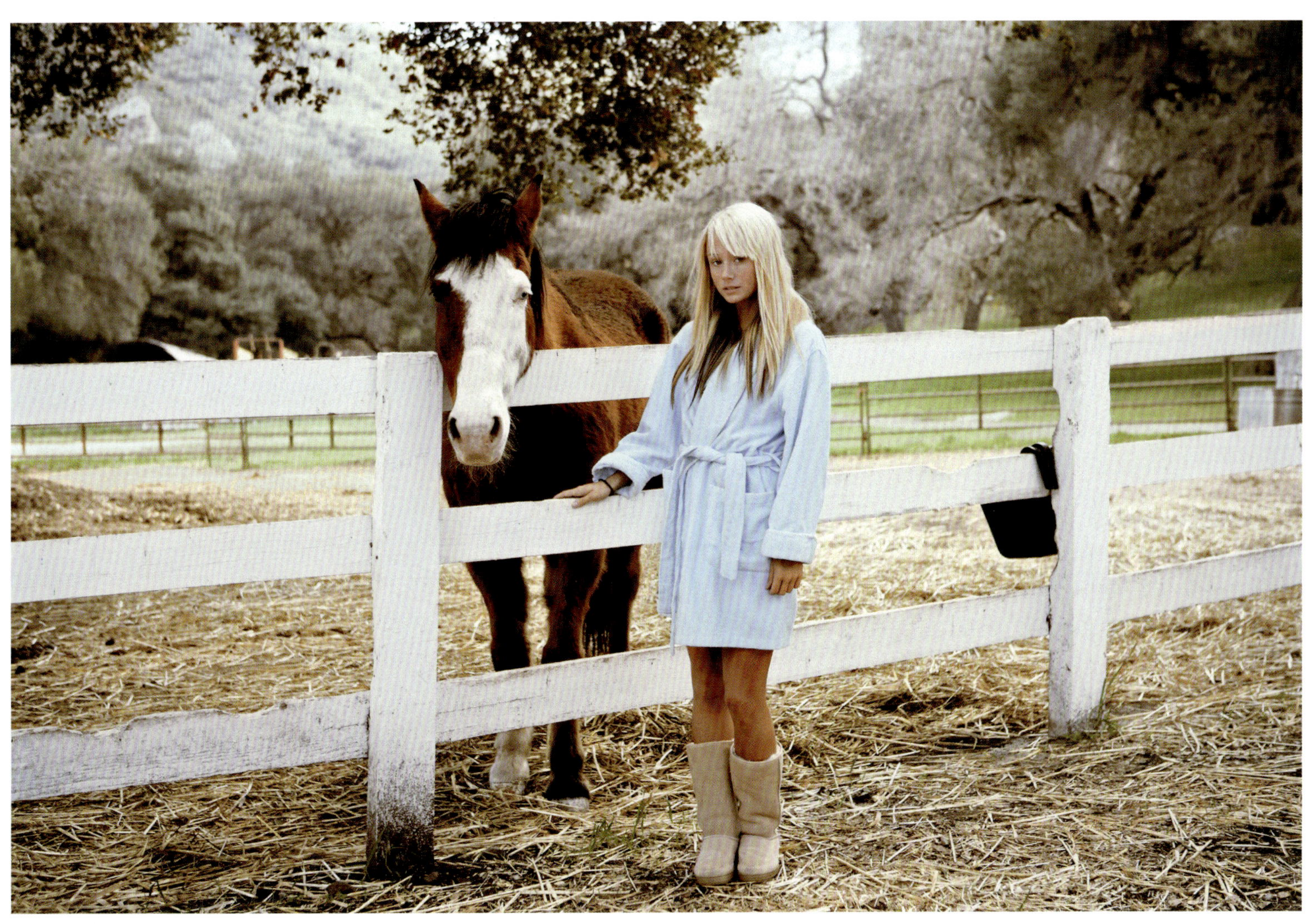

Michael Donald

Alex 'Hurricane' Higgins
November 2006

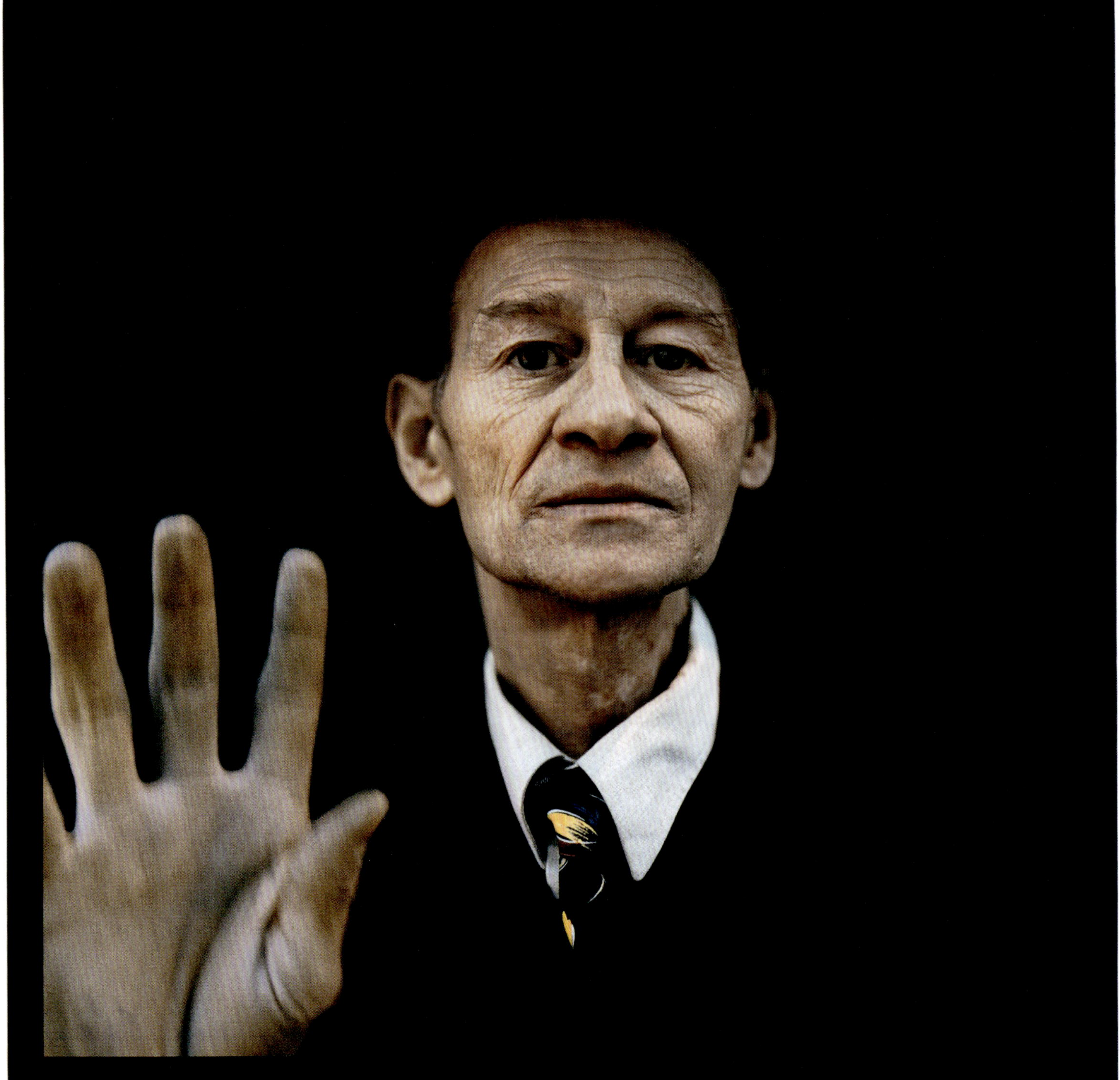

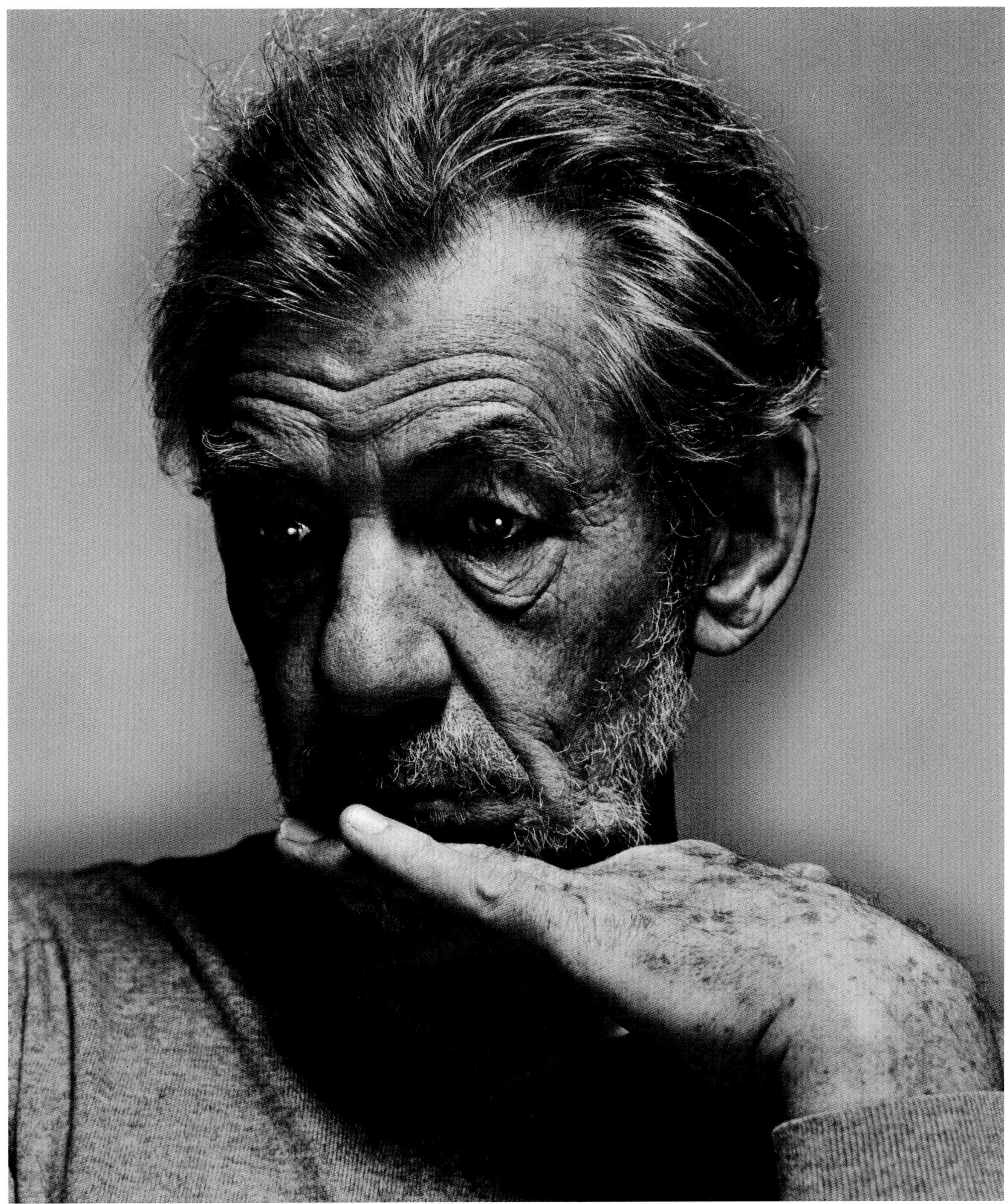

Jean Pascal Zahn

Young Woman
Playing the Piano
June 2007

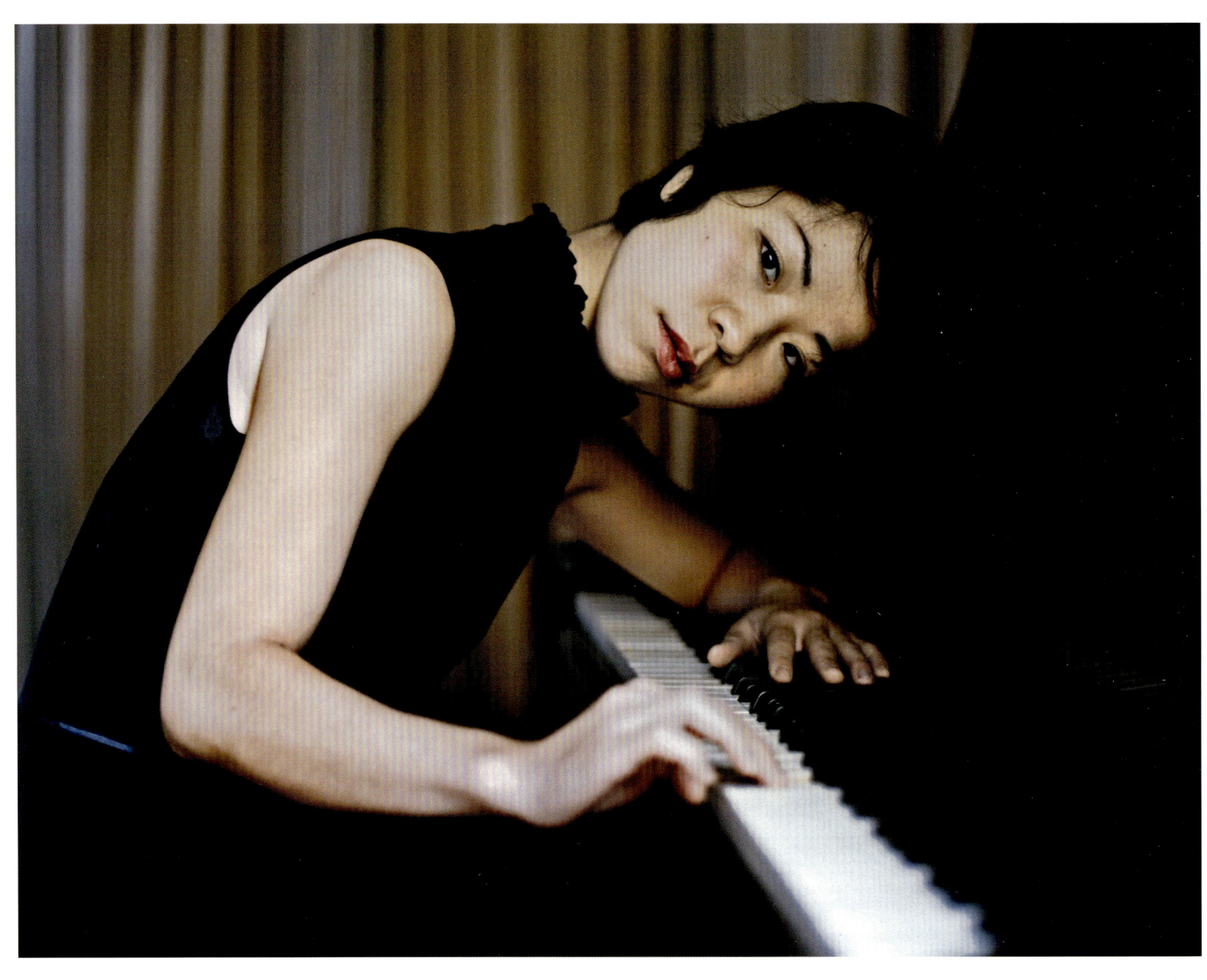

June 2006

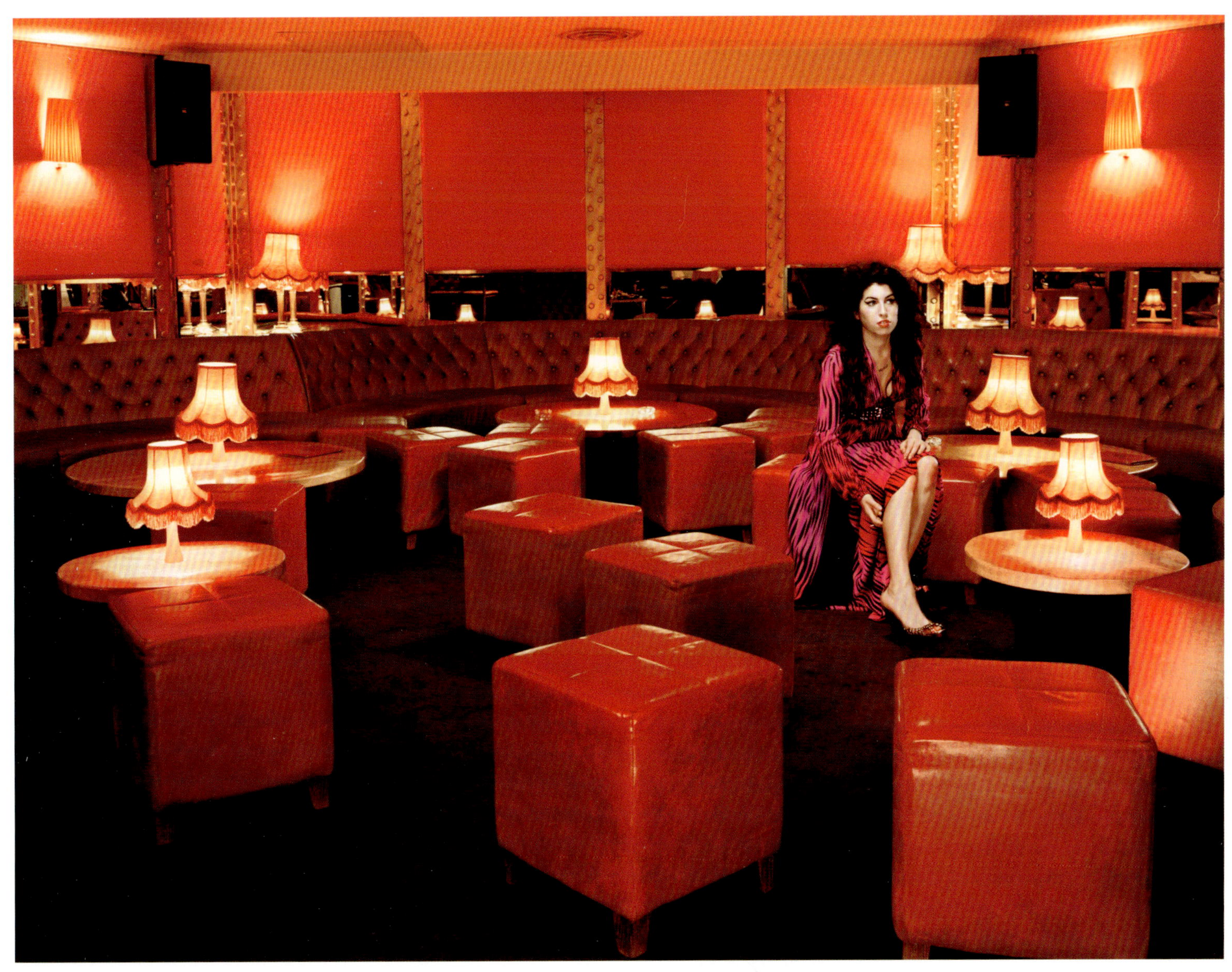

Lucy Levene

Mark
from the series
Marrying In
(Please God by You)
February 2007

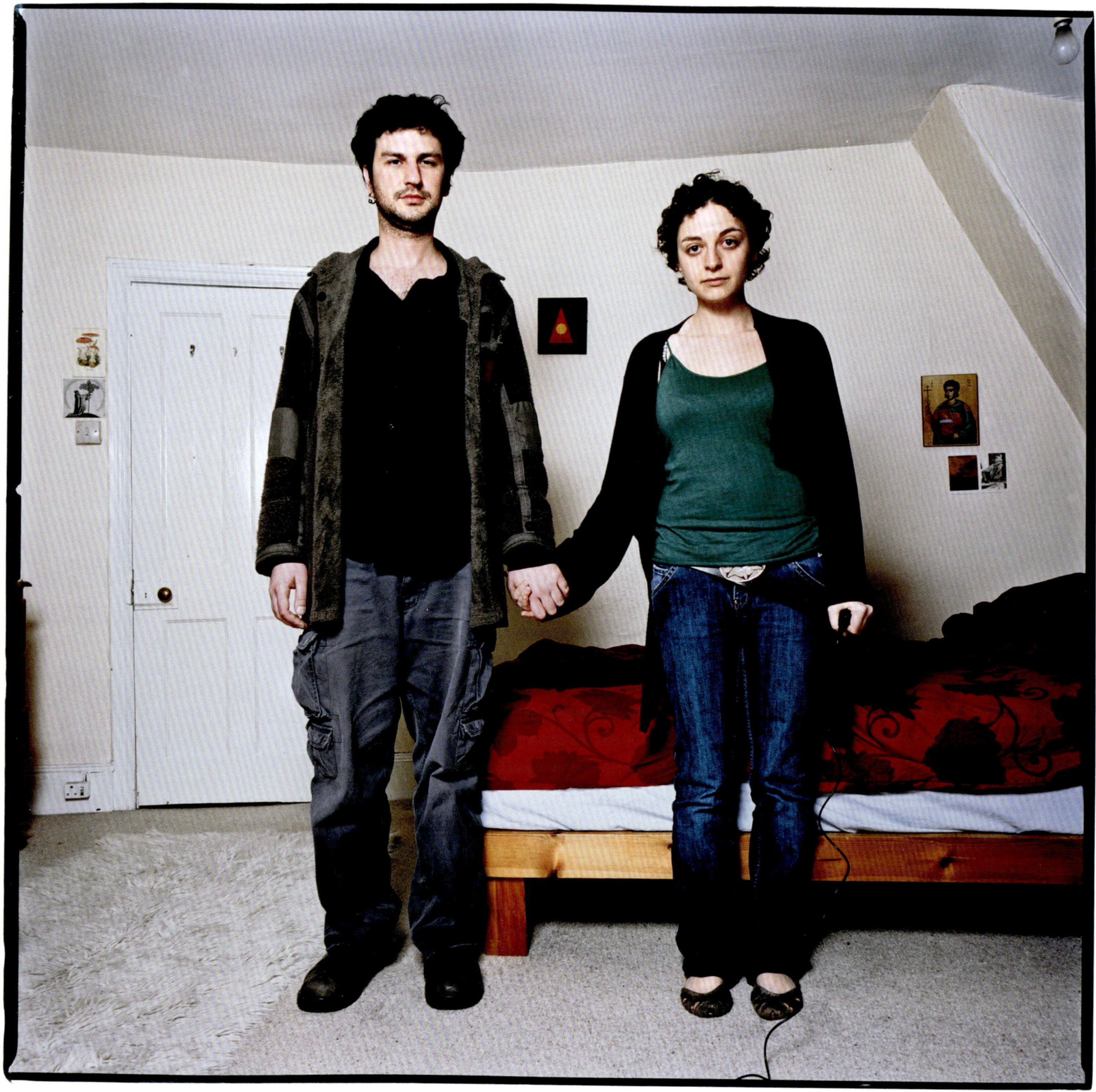

Frederic Huska

Beth
April 2007

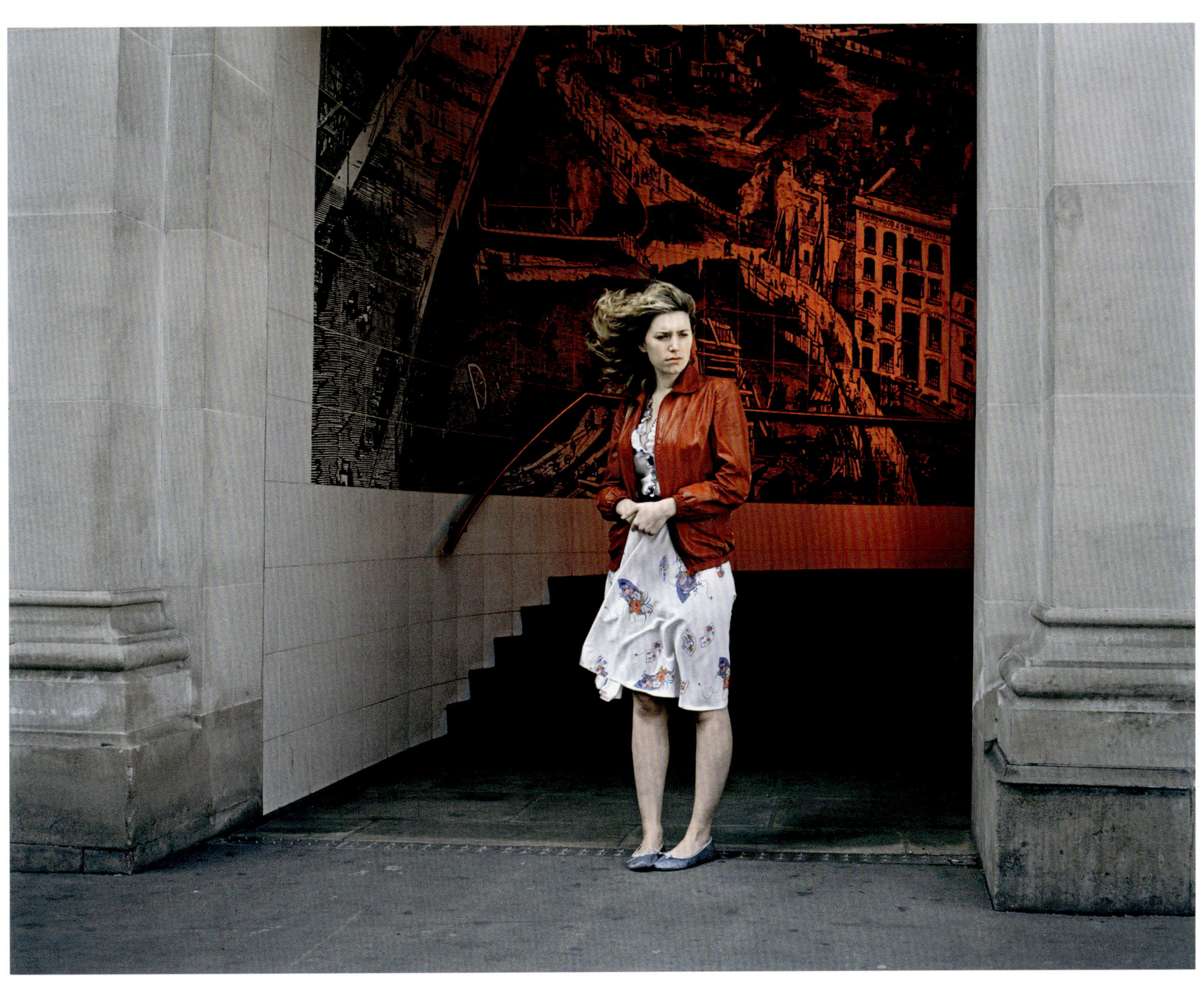

Sophia
September 2006

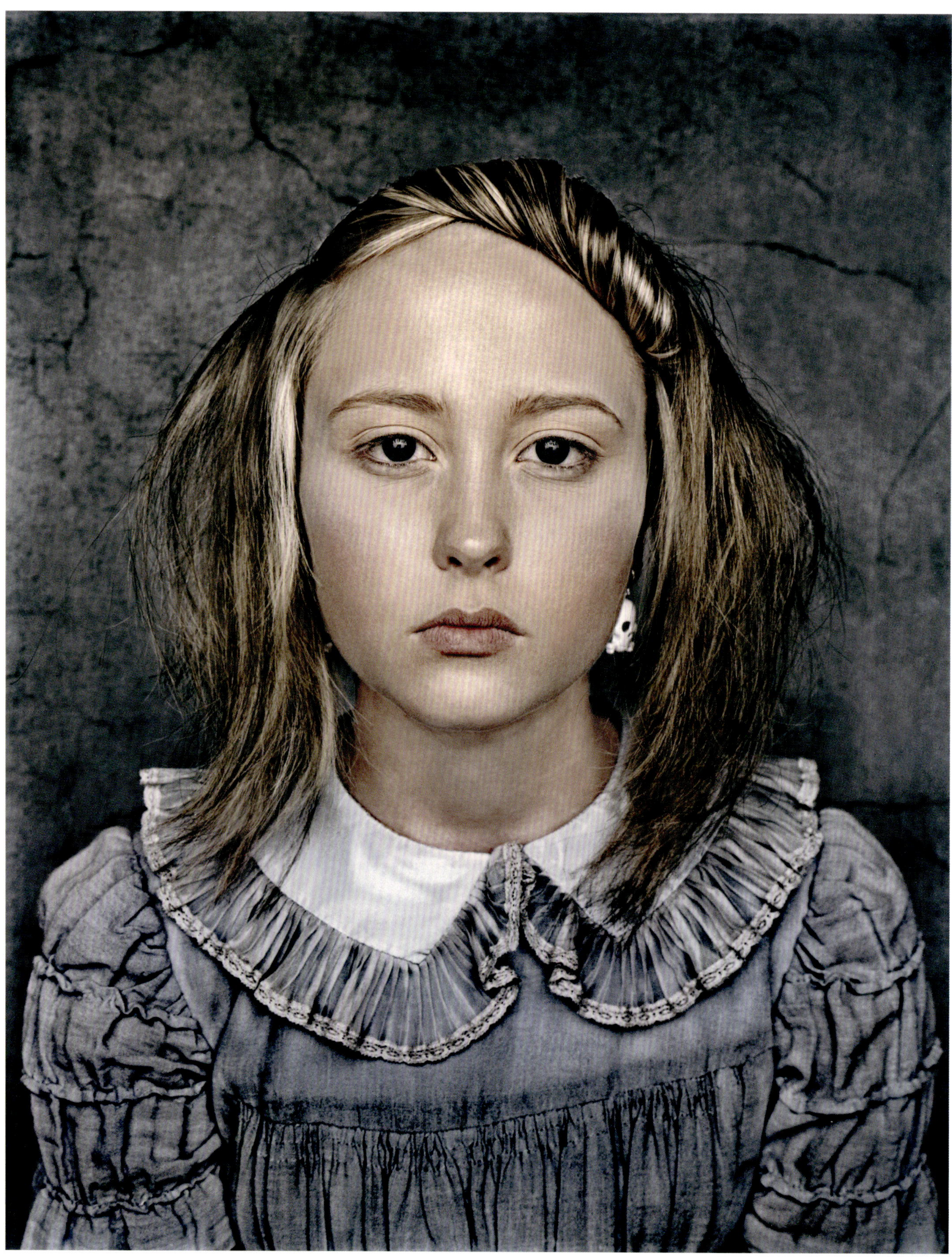

Eric Klemm

Linda, Haudenasaune Woman, Florida *from the series*

Silent Warriors – Portraits of North American Indians
November 2006

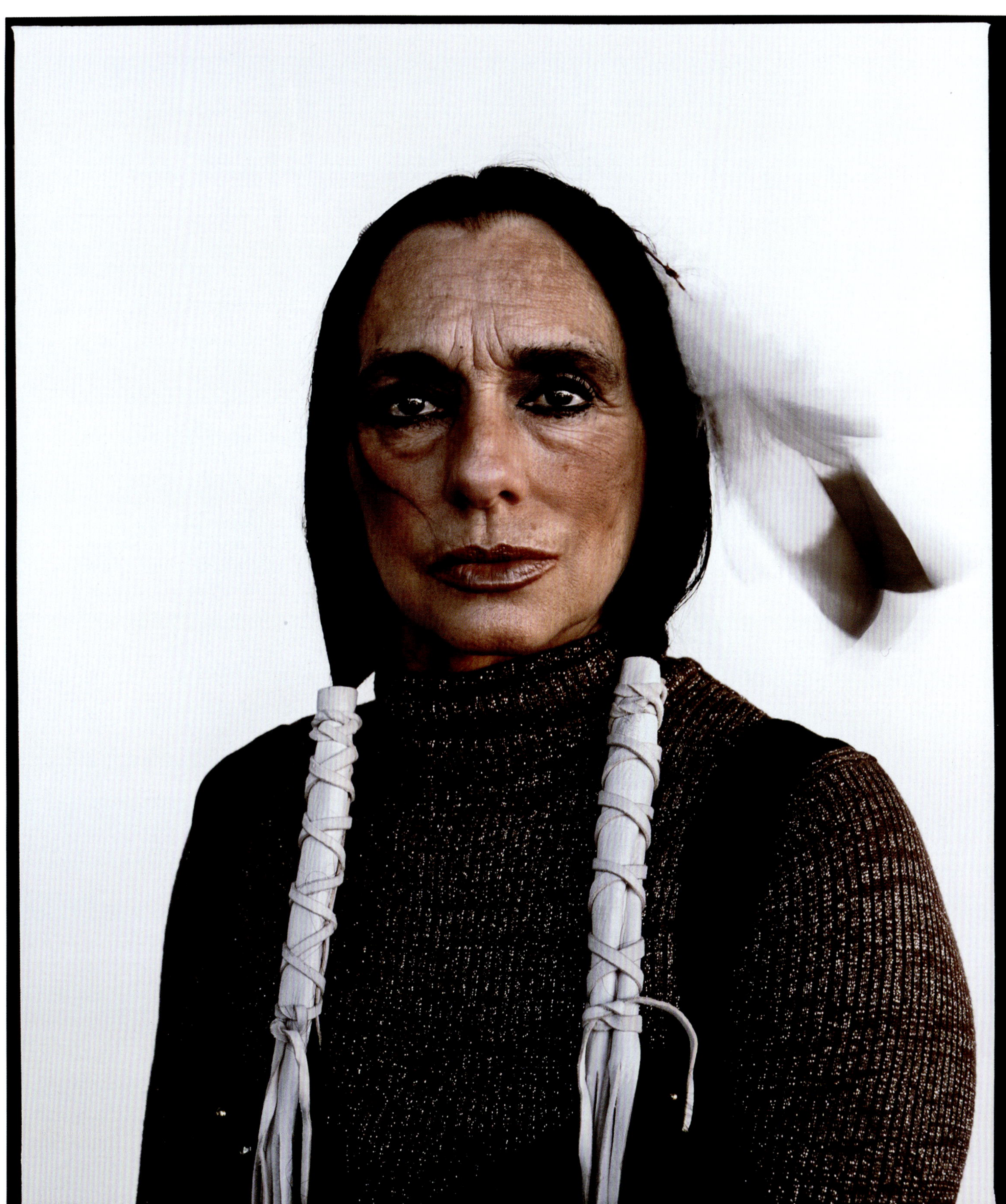

Mark Oliver

Kids in the Garden
of Princess Mafalda
von Hessen
from the series
Princess Mafalda
von Hessen
Story for AD
September 2006

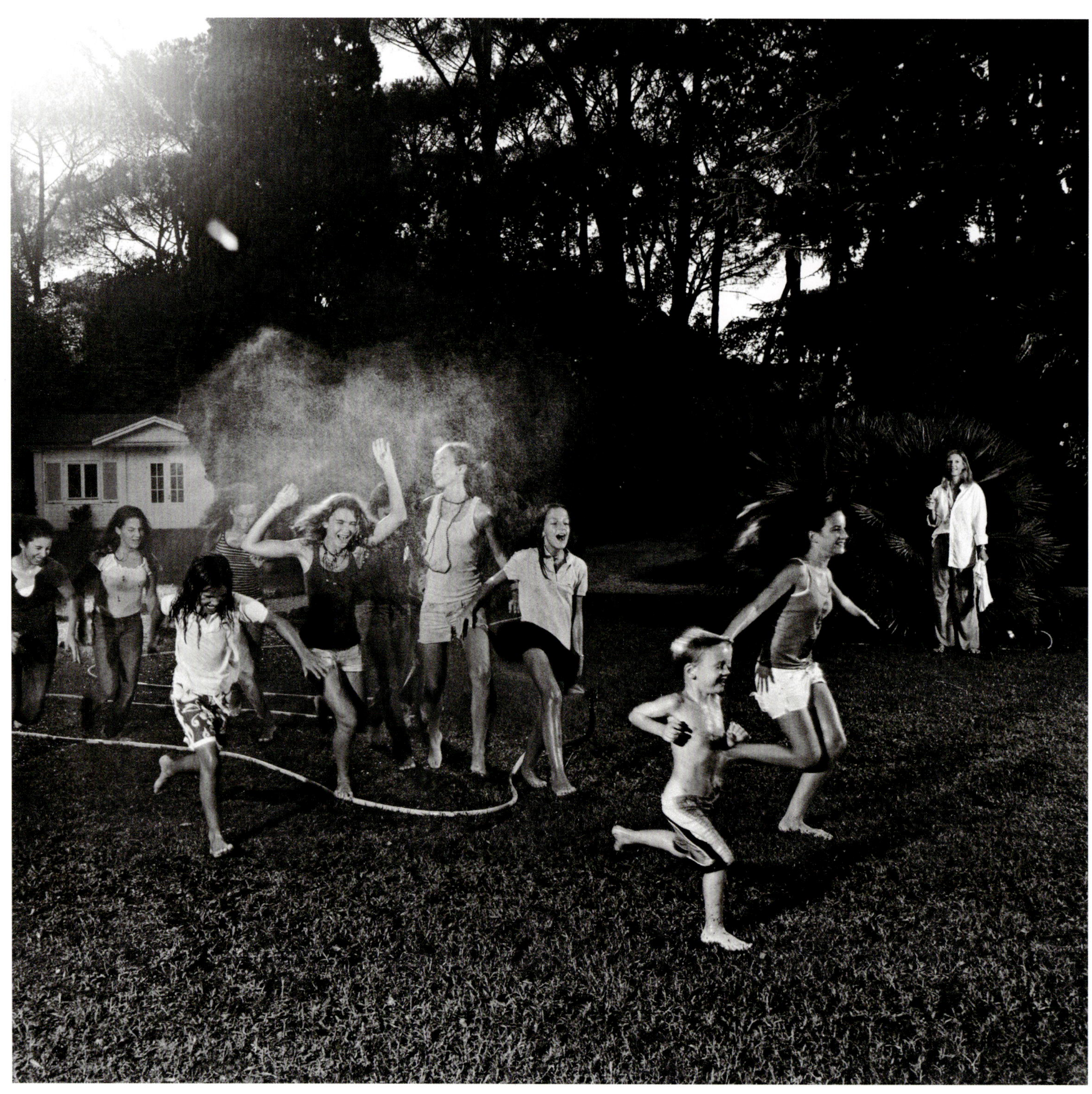

Ozlem
August 2006

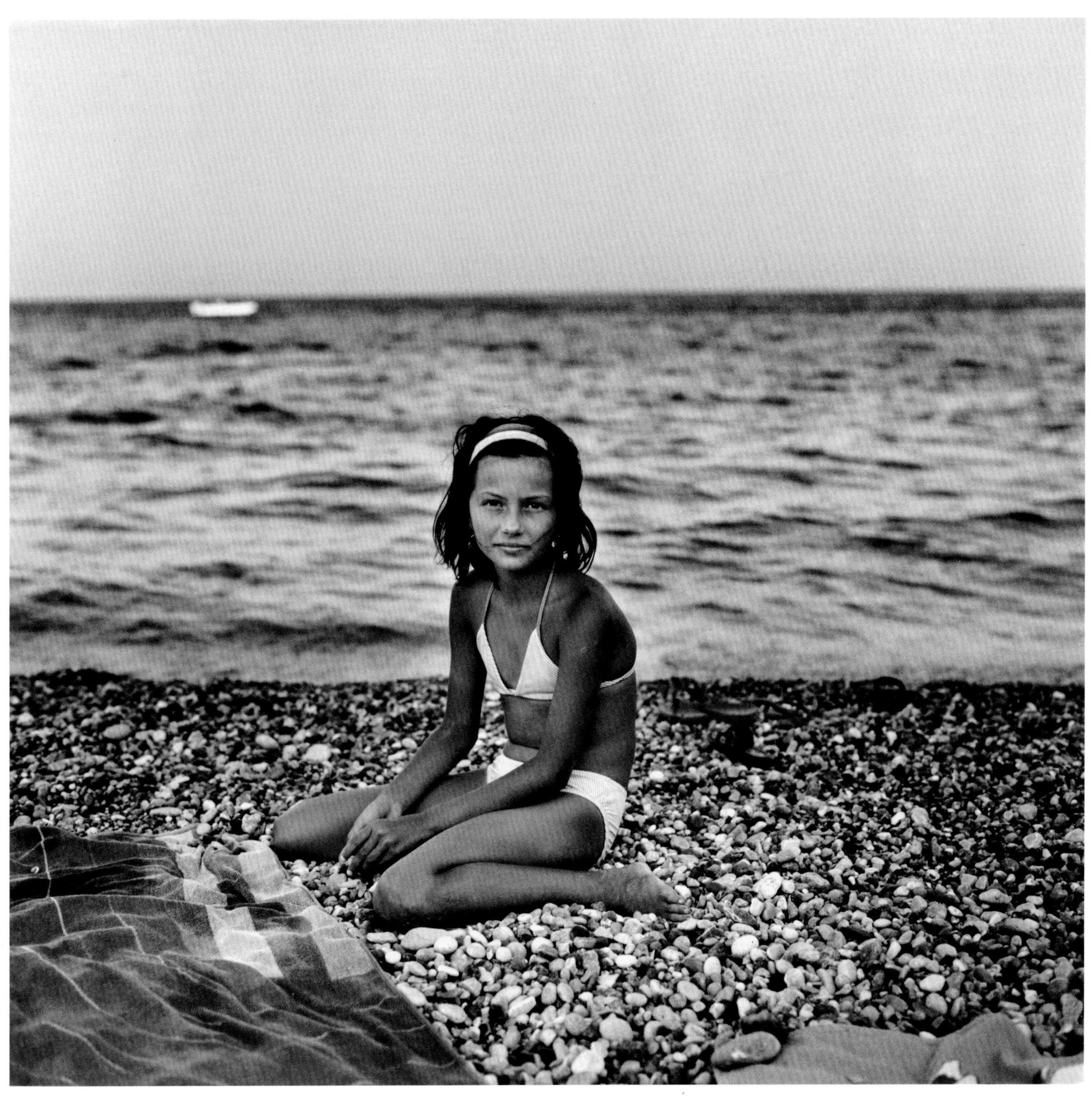

Shara Henderson

Lily-Pea
December 2006

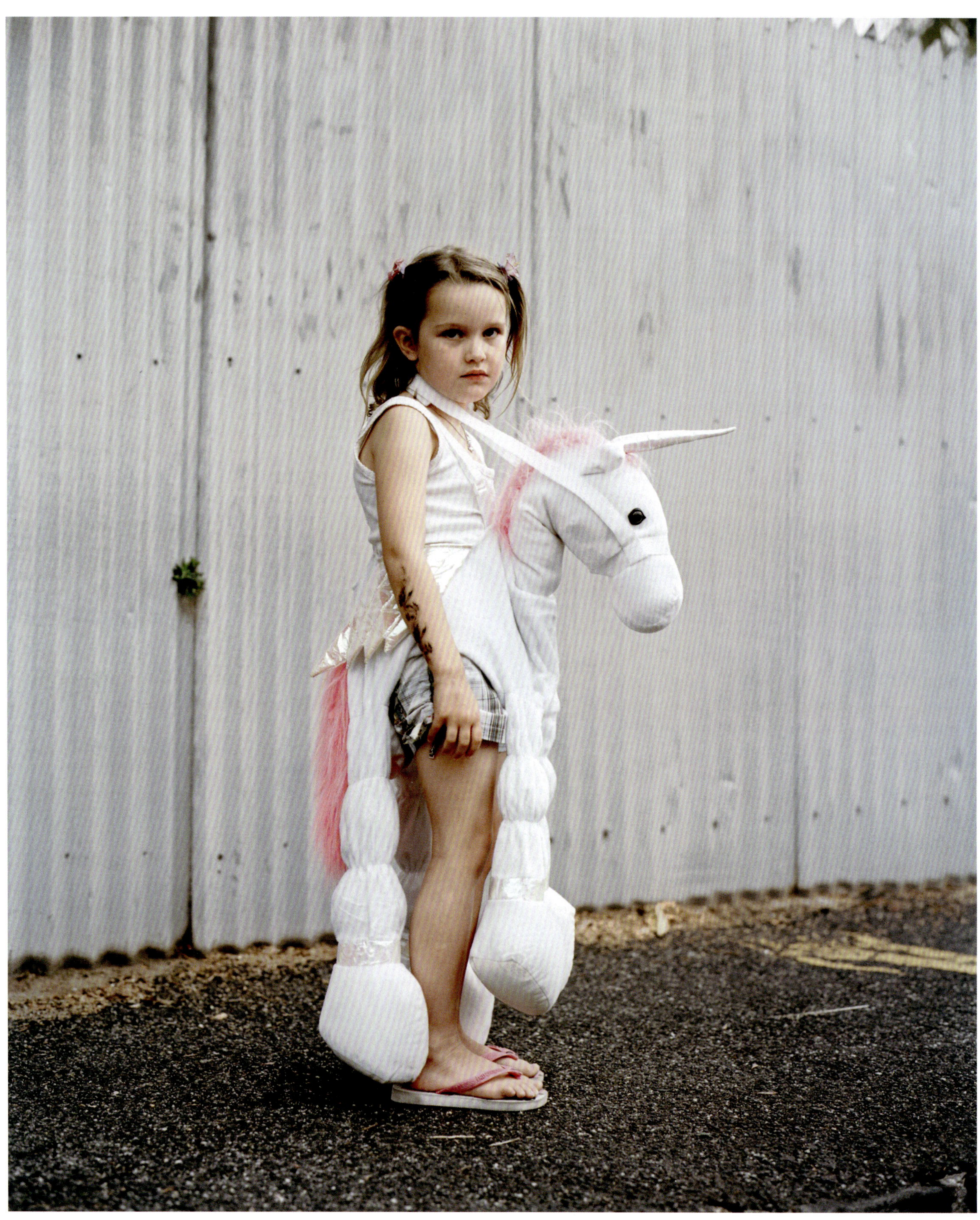

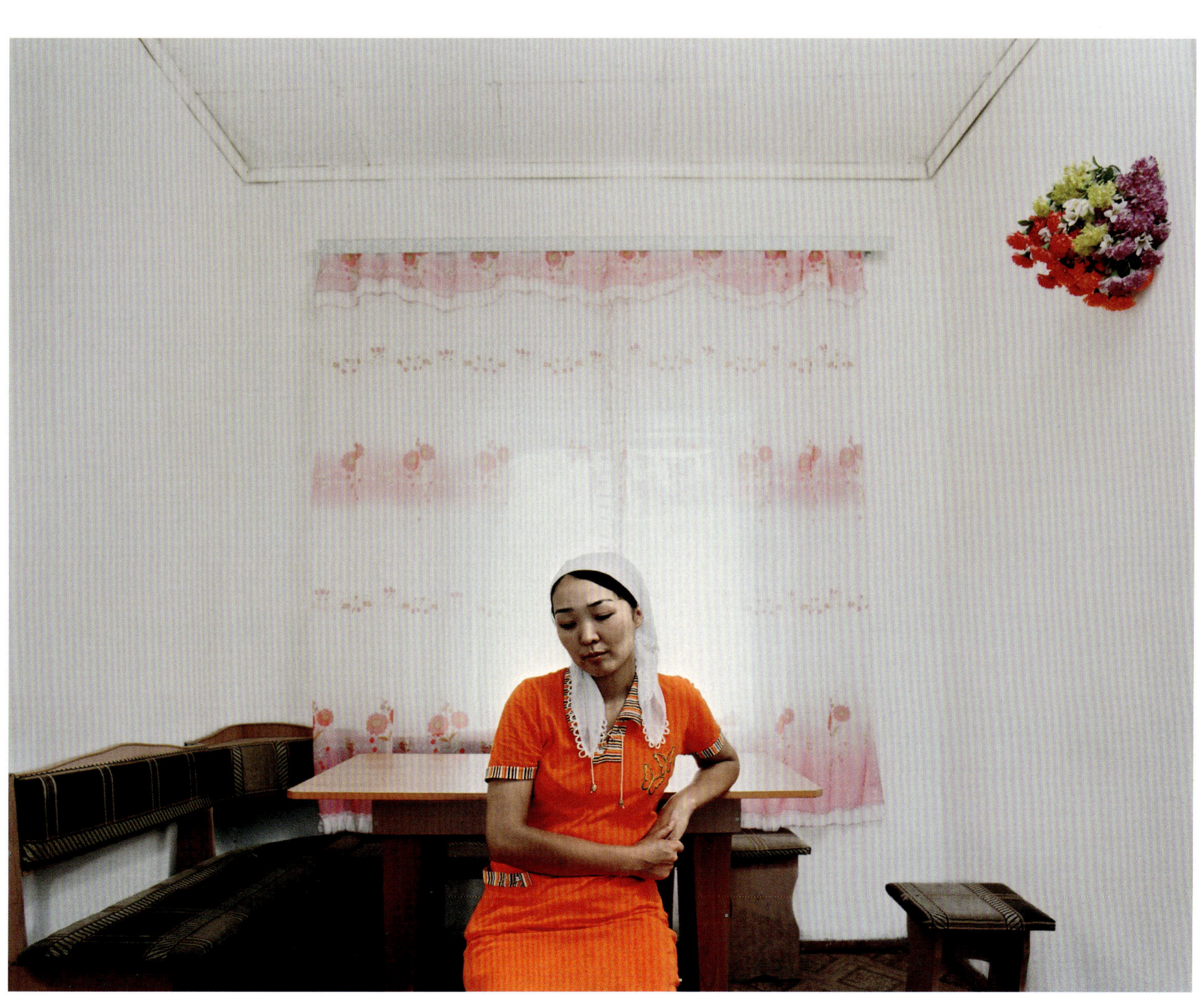

Niamh – Age 11
April 2007

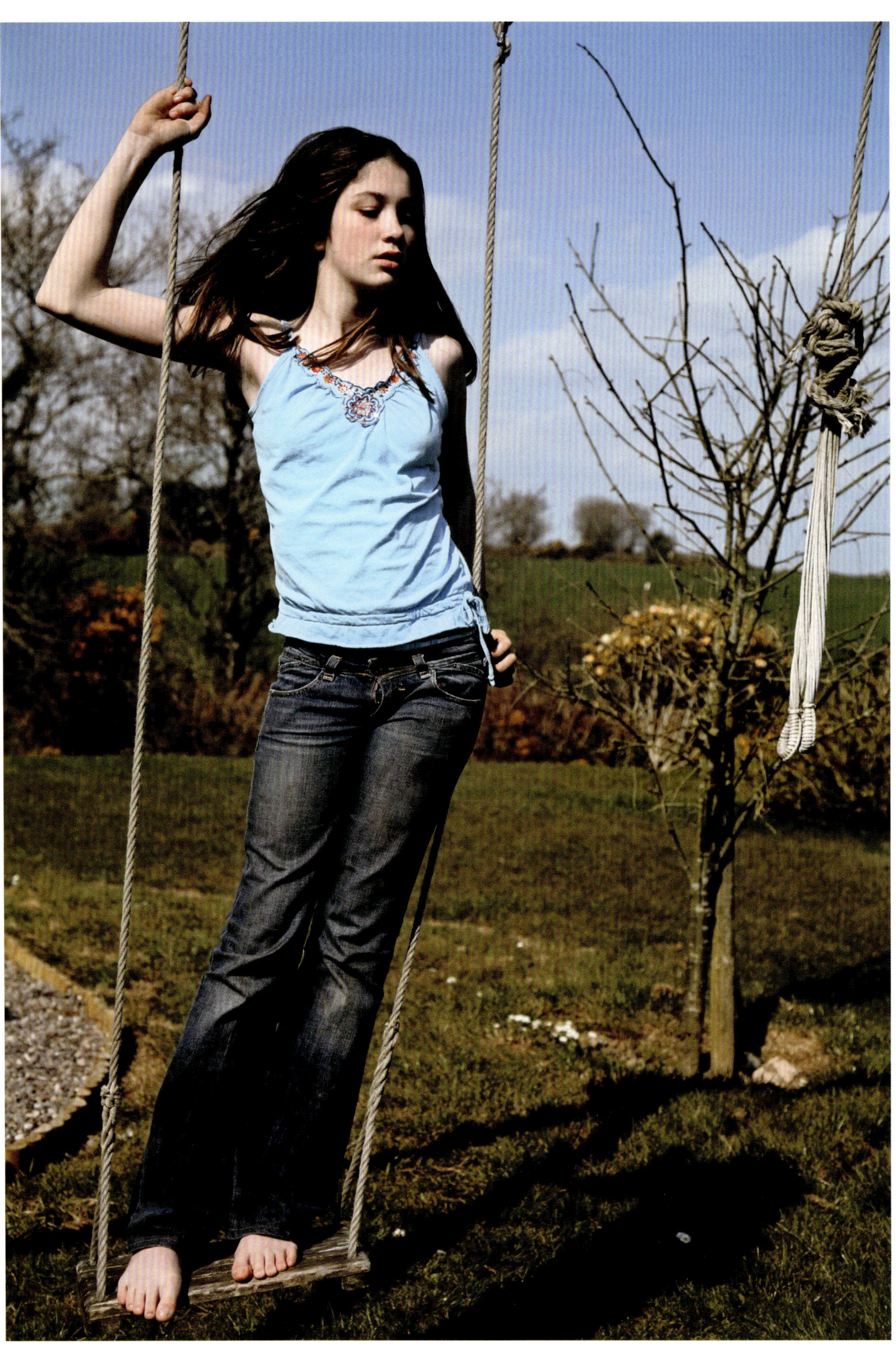

Michael Jones

Kids
from the series
The Commute
June 2007

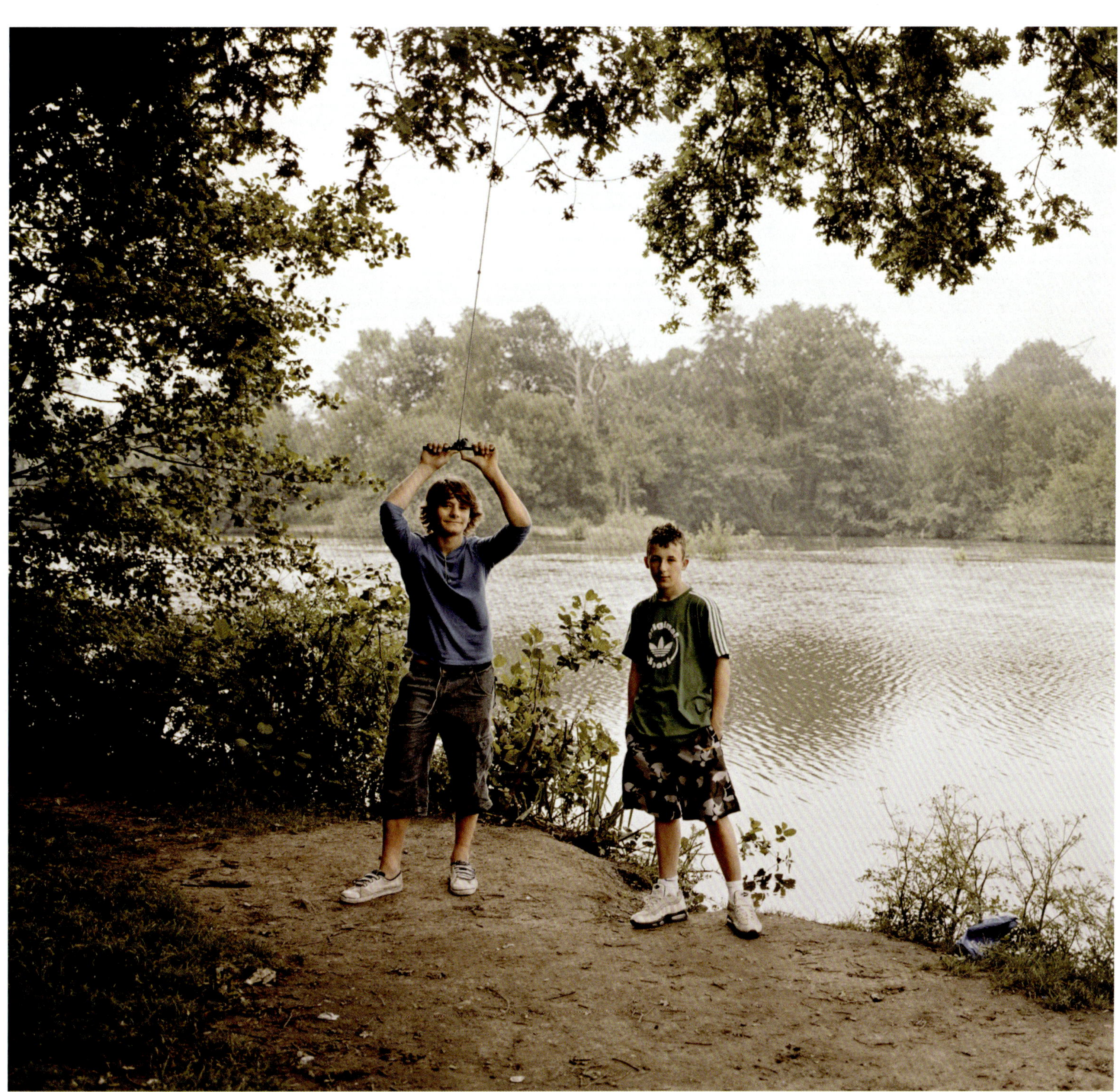

Michal Chelbin

'Black Eye',
Ukraine 2006
from the series
Strangely Familiar
June 2006

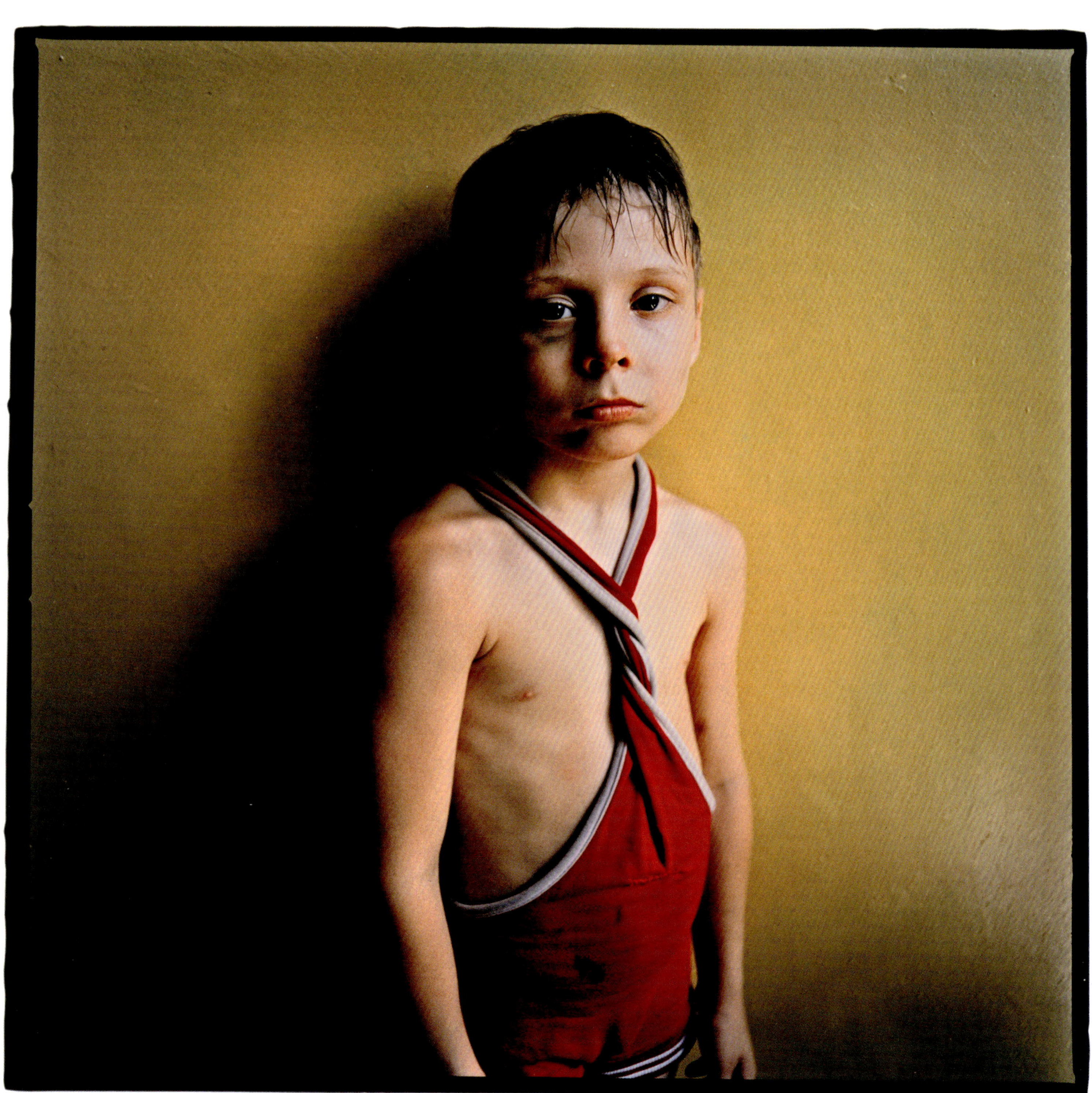

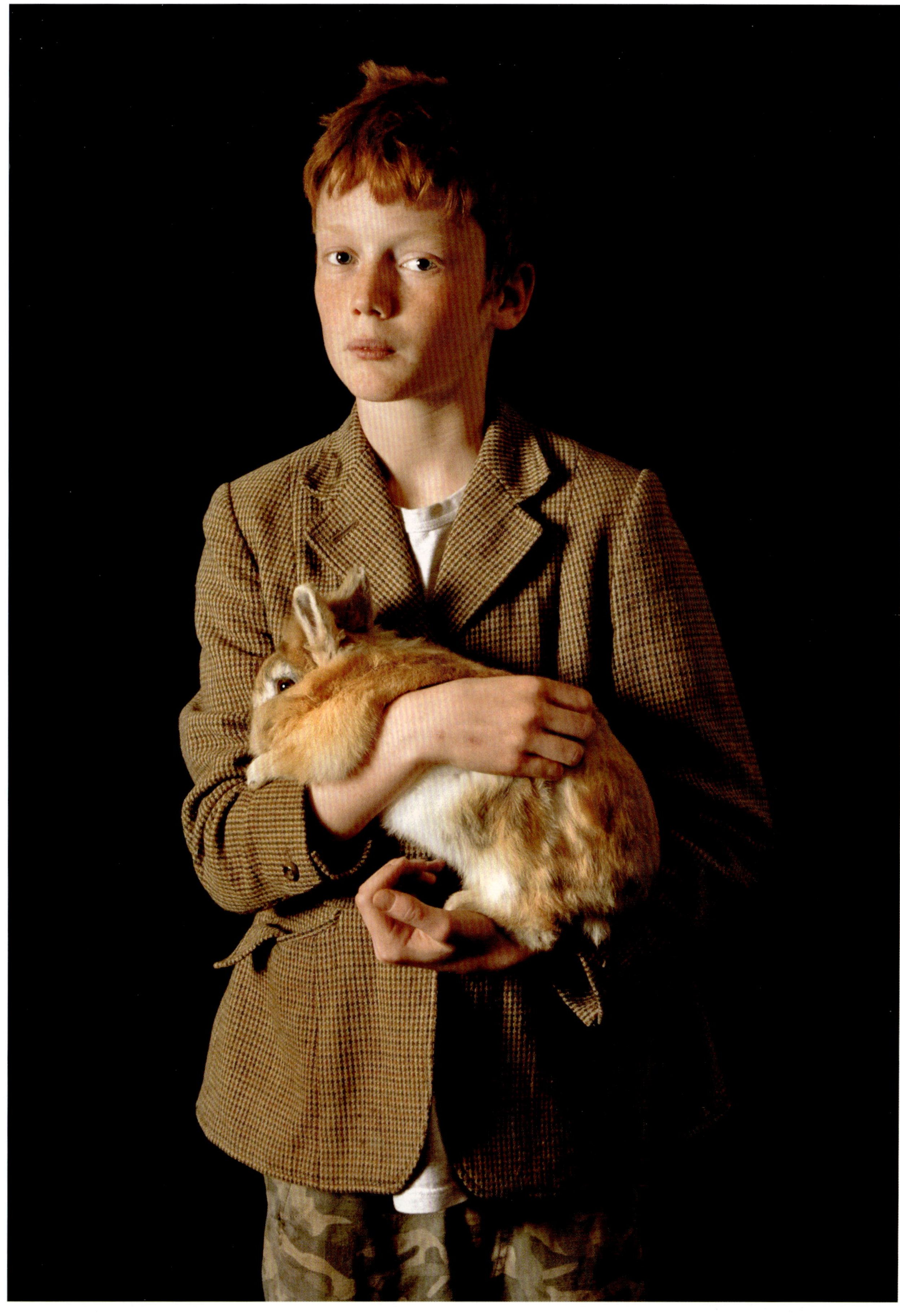

Mother and Daughter
June 2007

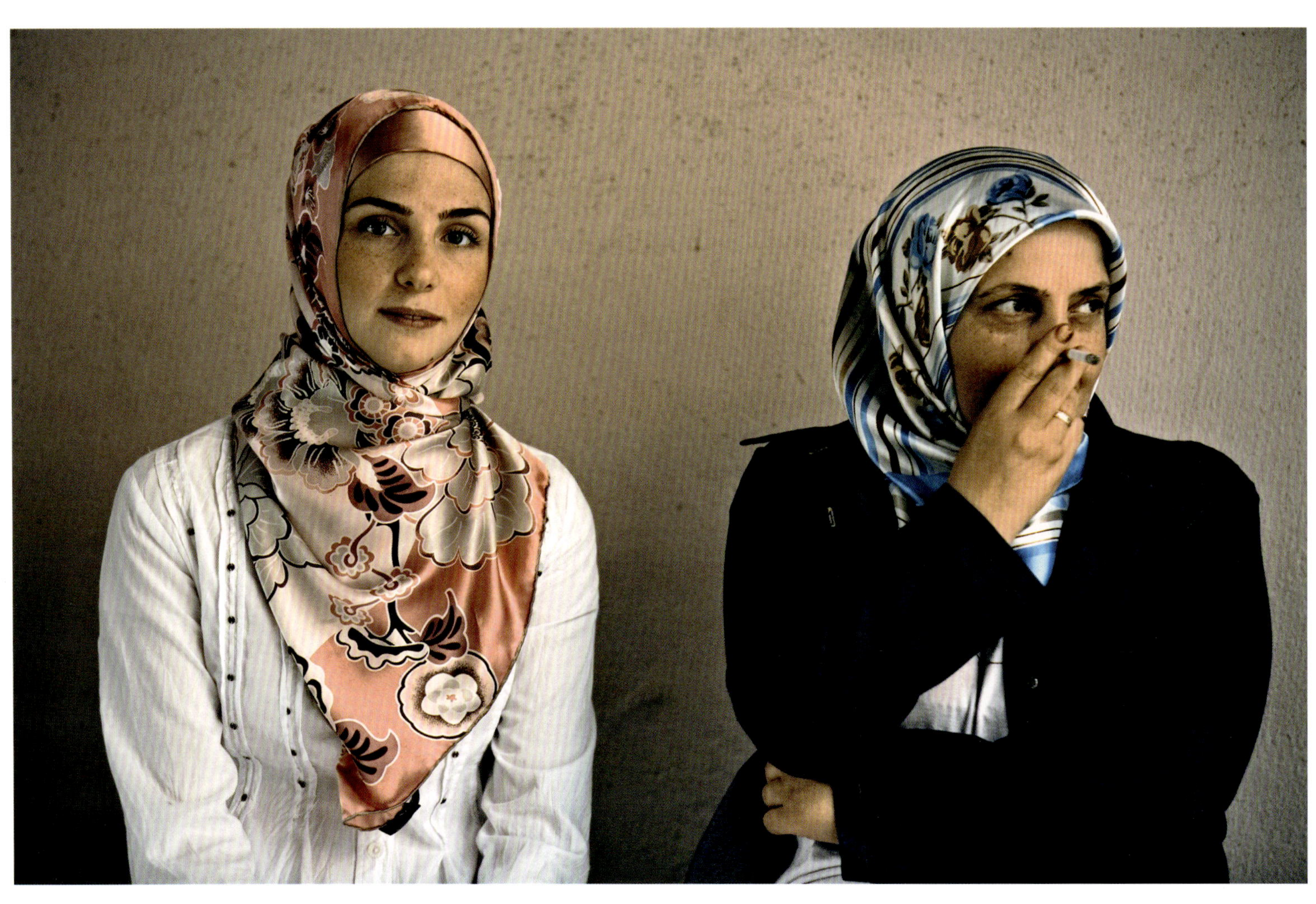

Juan Pedro Trejo

Malena
from the series
Almario
December 2006

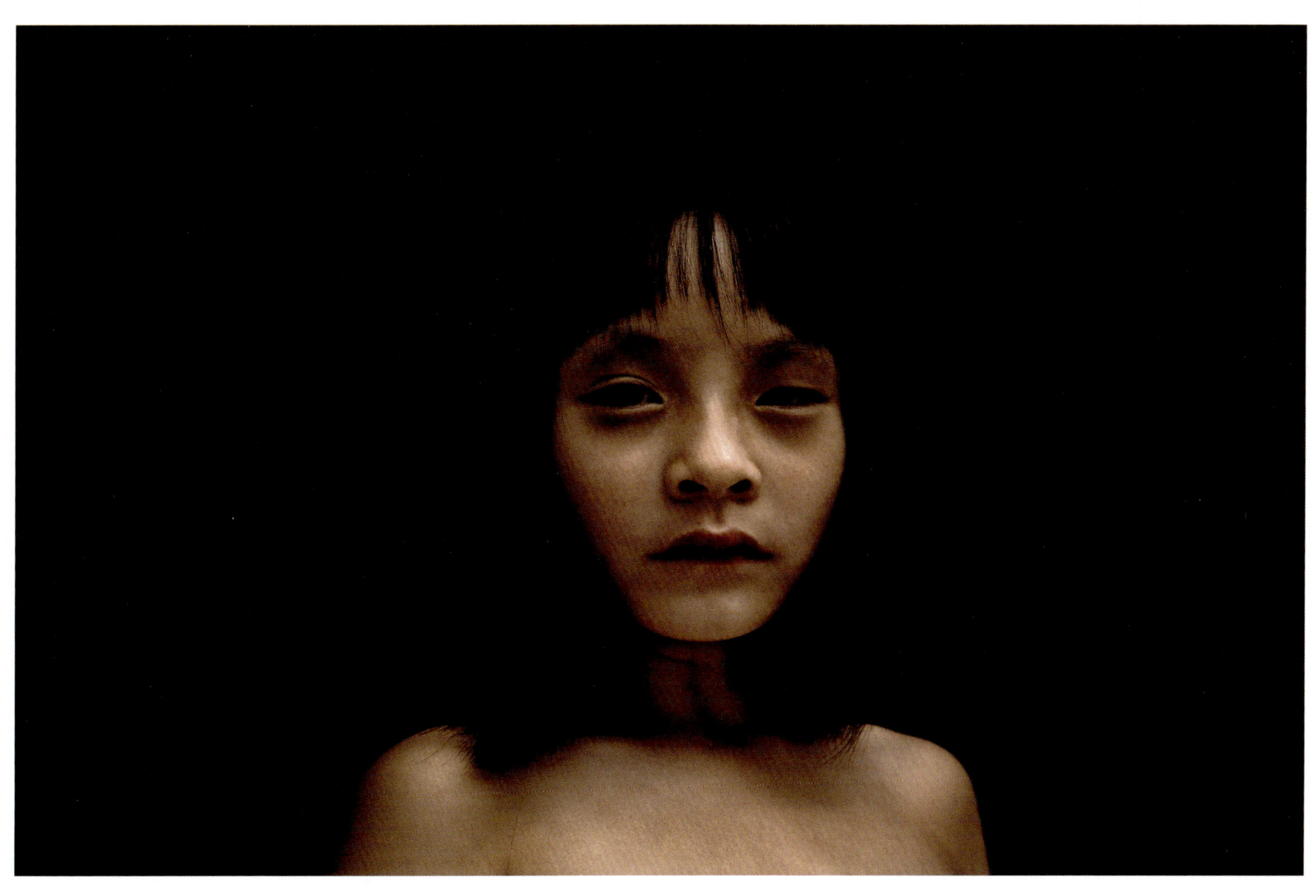

Ric Bower

Jan, Kayleigh and Kizzie
from the series

Xmas Blingers
December 2006

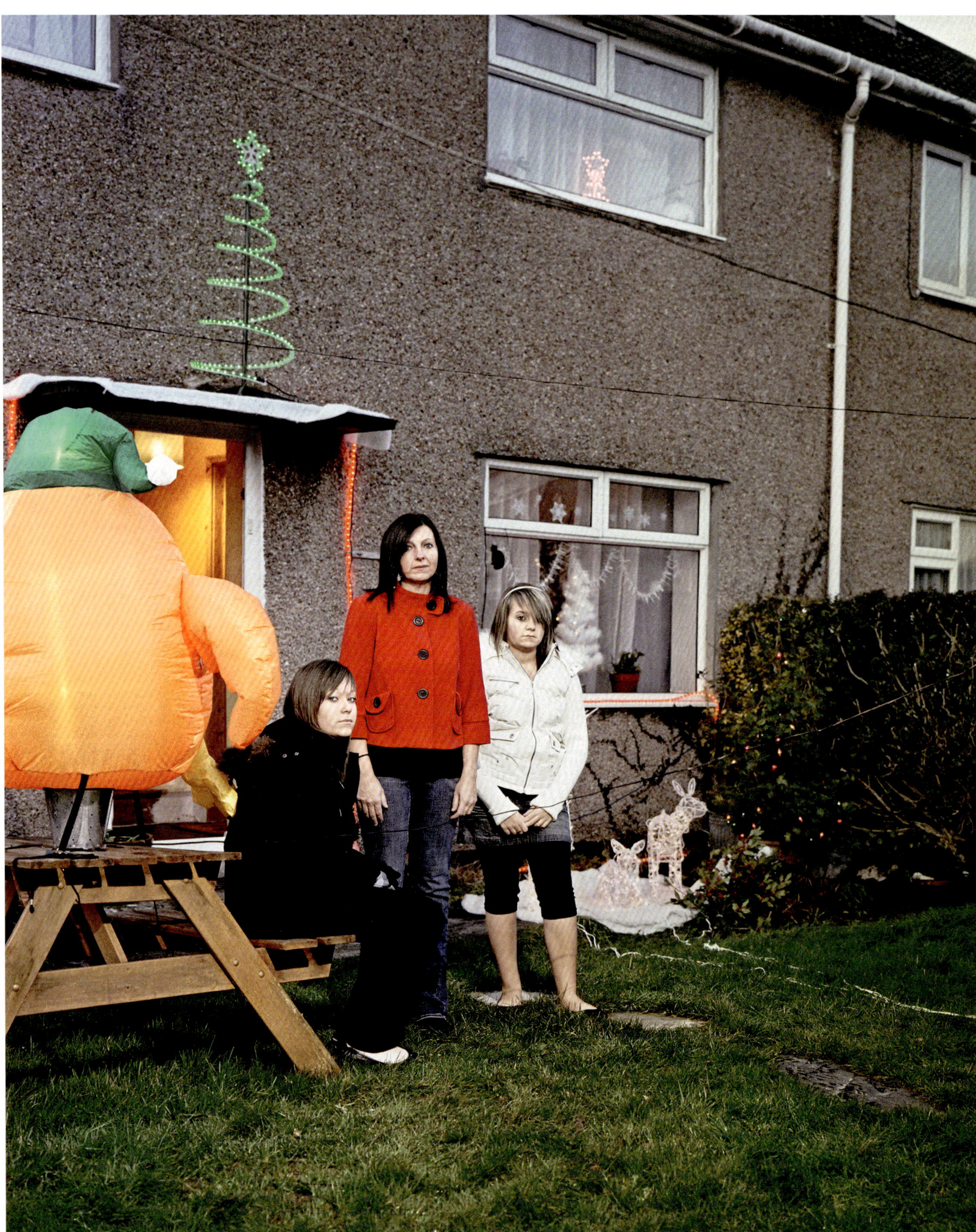

Philippe Pleasants

Croydon, London
from the series
Night Portraits
July 2006

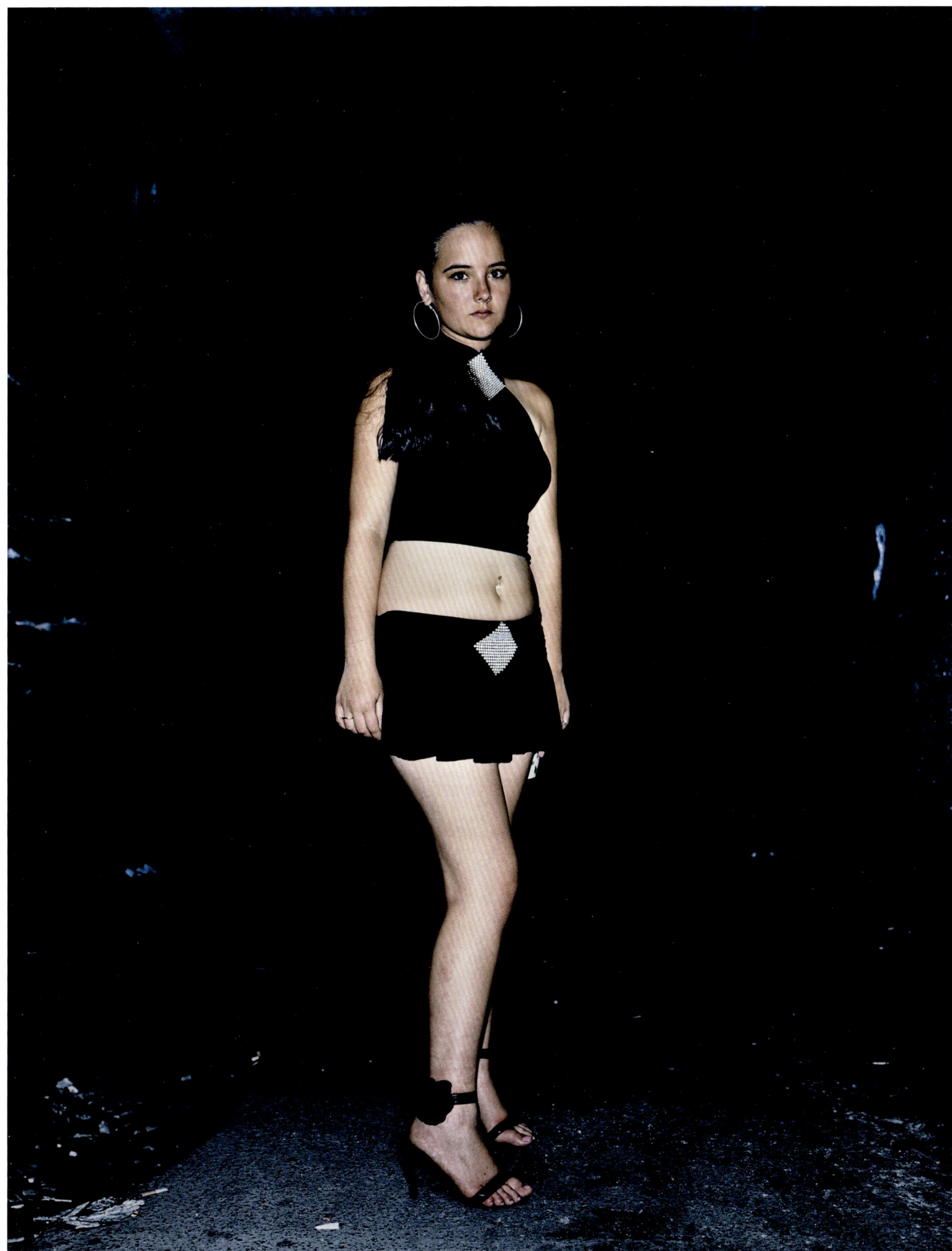

Niko von Glasow
and Ania Dabrowska

Kim Morton
from the series
NoBody's Perfect
May 2007

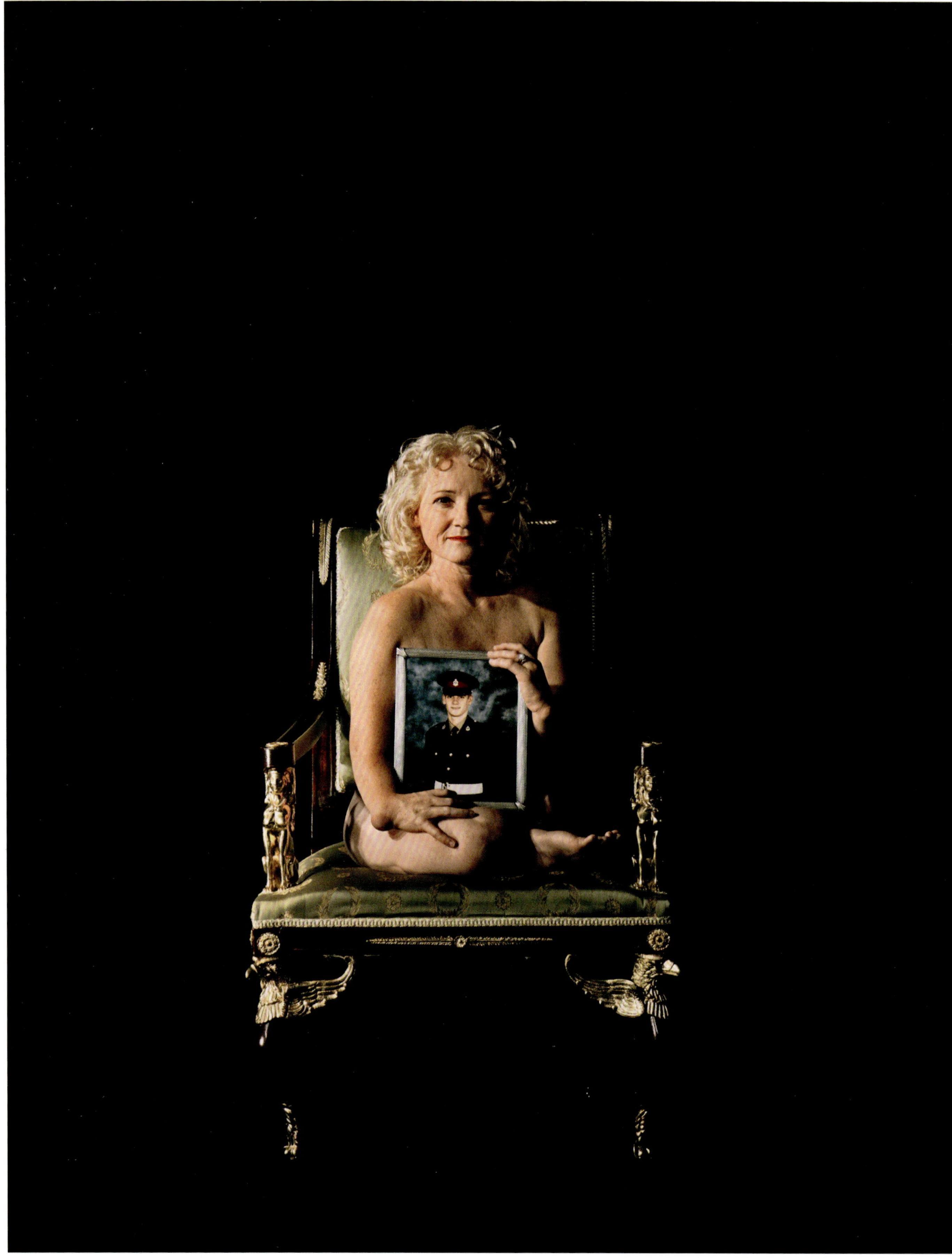

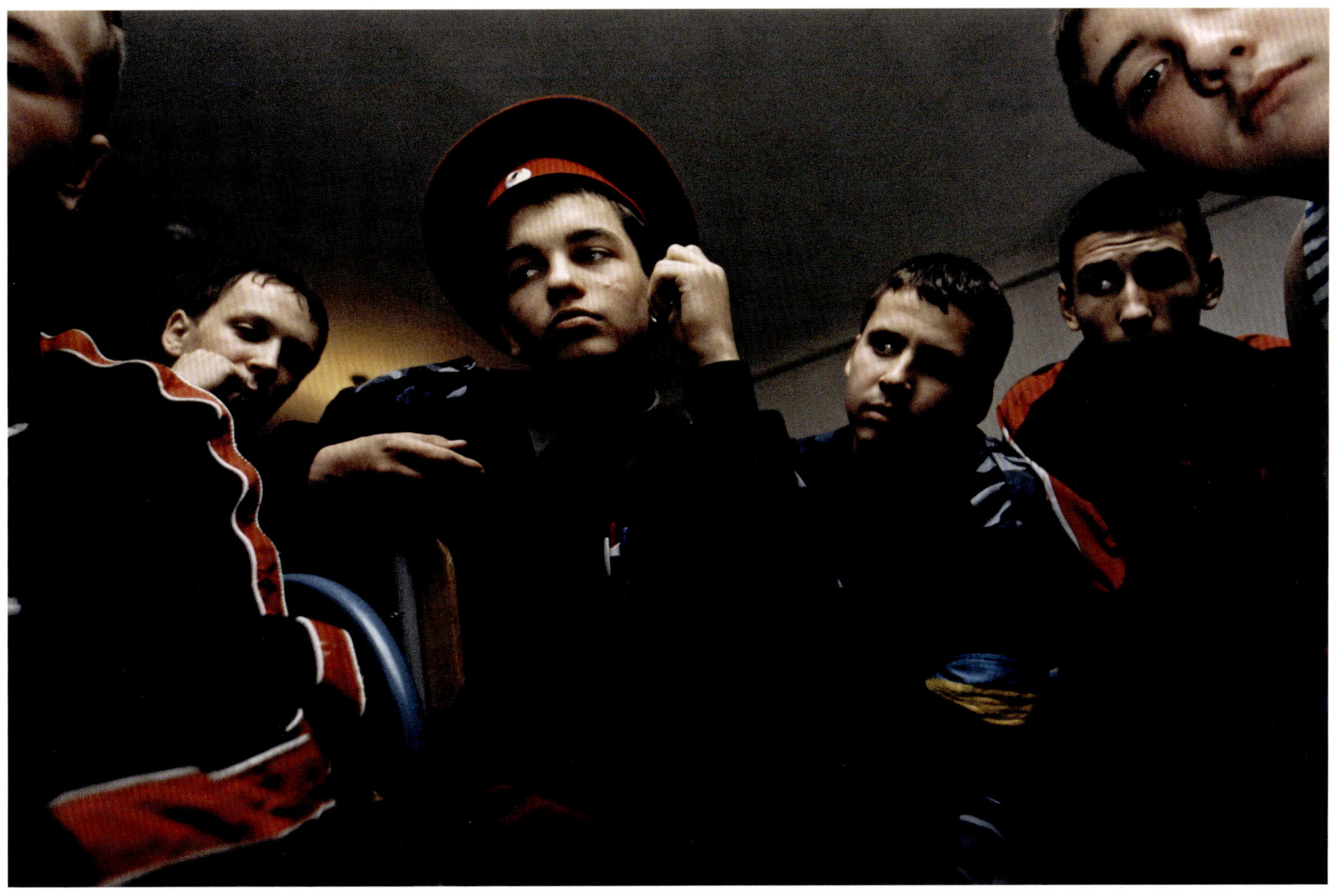

Tim Walker

Otis Ferry and his Hunting Hounds
May 2007

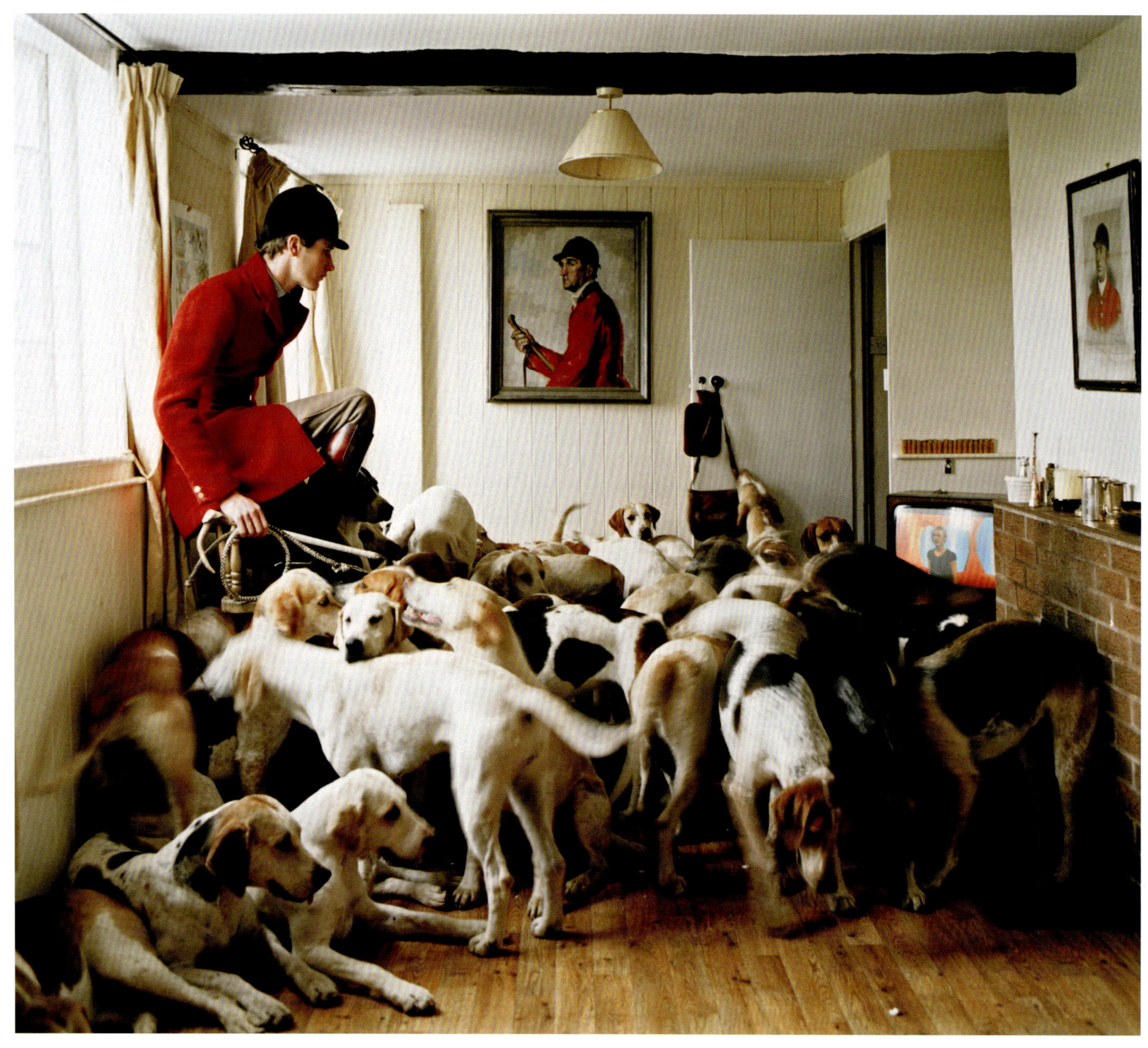

Chad Hunt

PFC Heather Ragan, 19, Oklahoma City *from the series* Young American Soldiers in Afghanistan October 2006

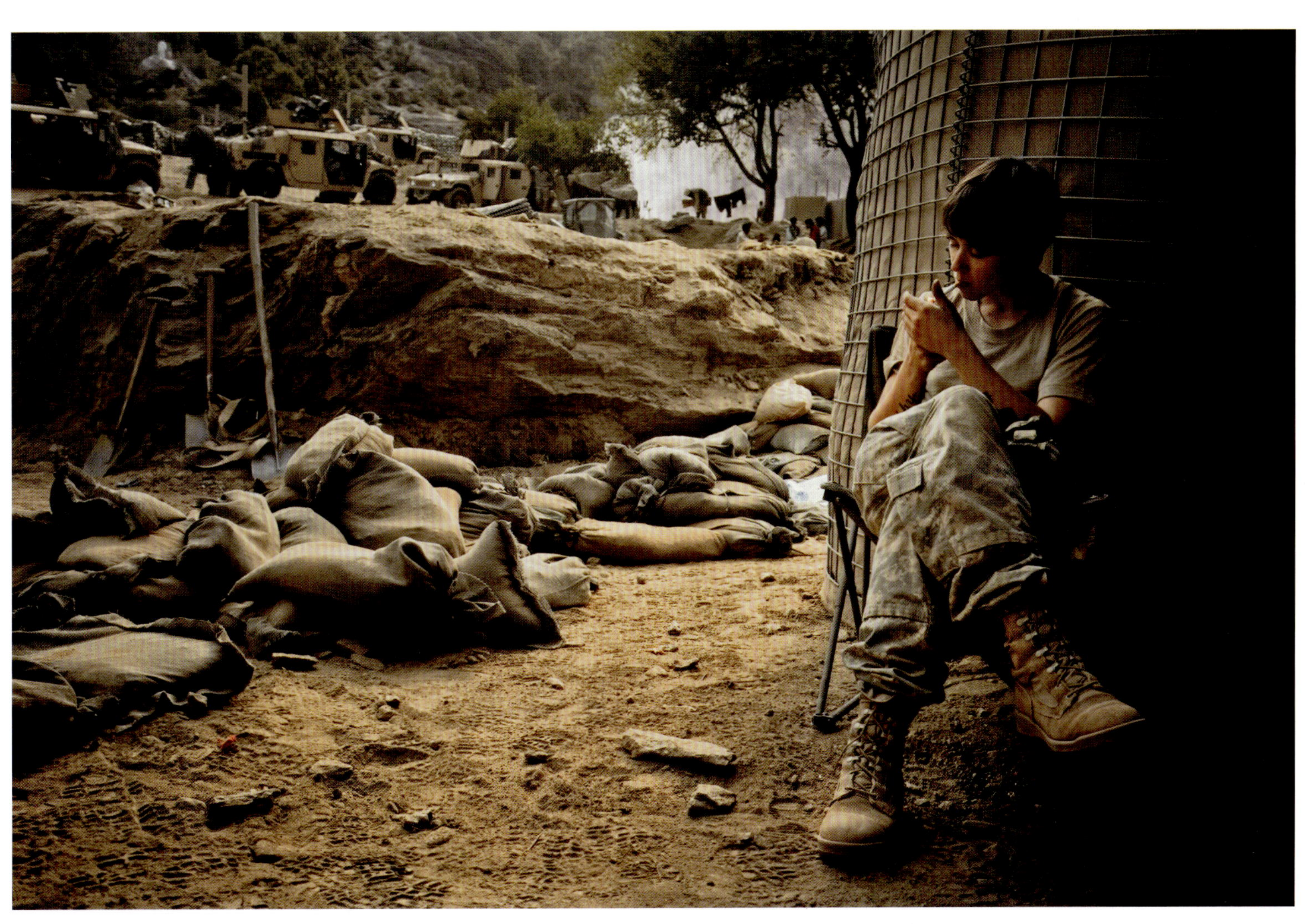

Kate Elliott

Untitled
from the series

Gypsy Horse Fair 1
October 2006

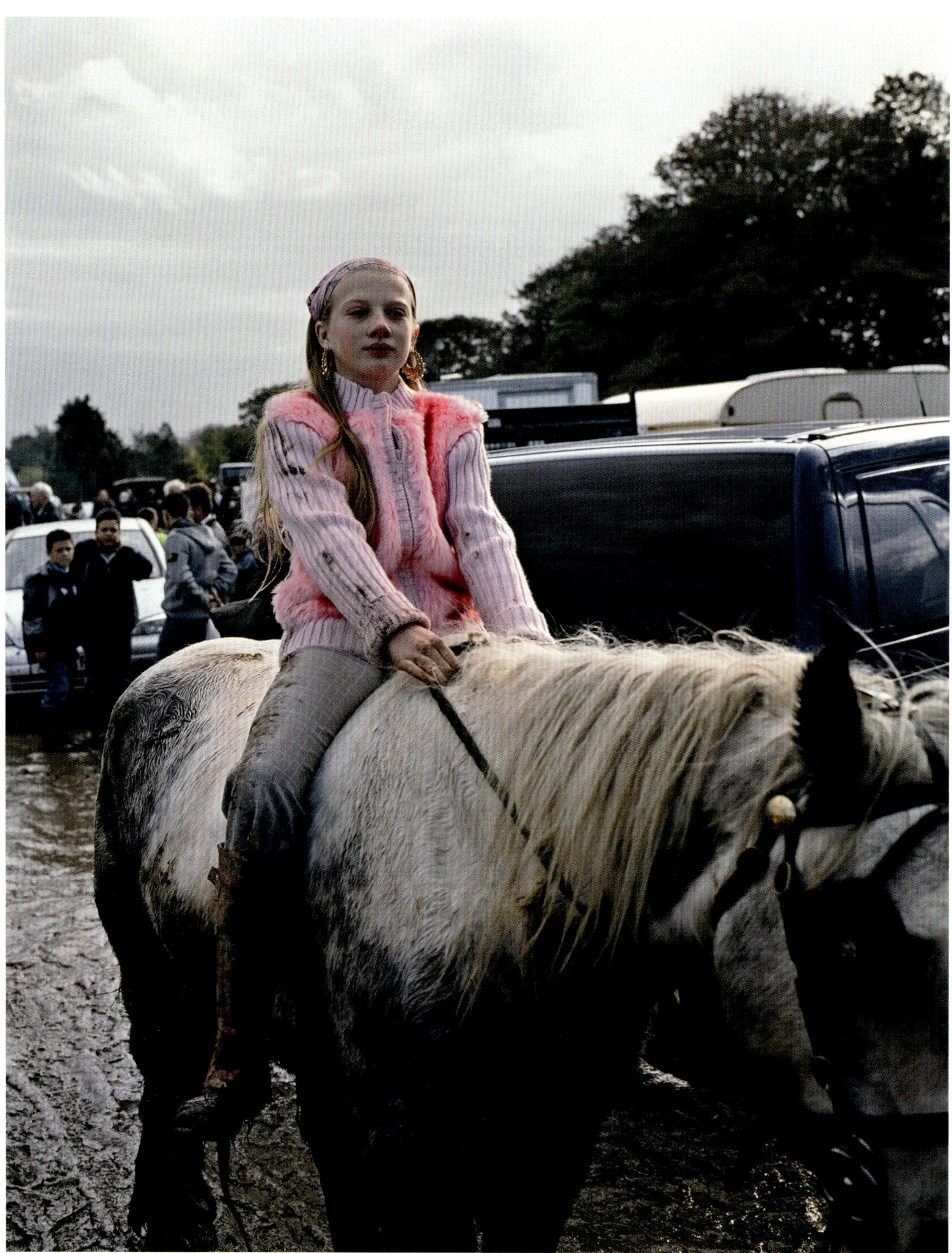

Harry Borden

Untitled
August 2006

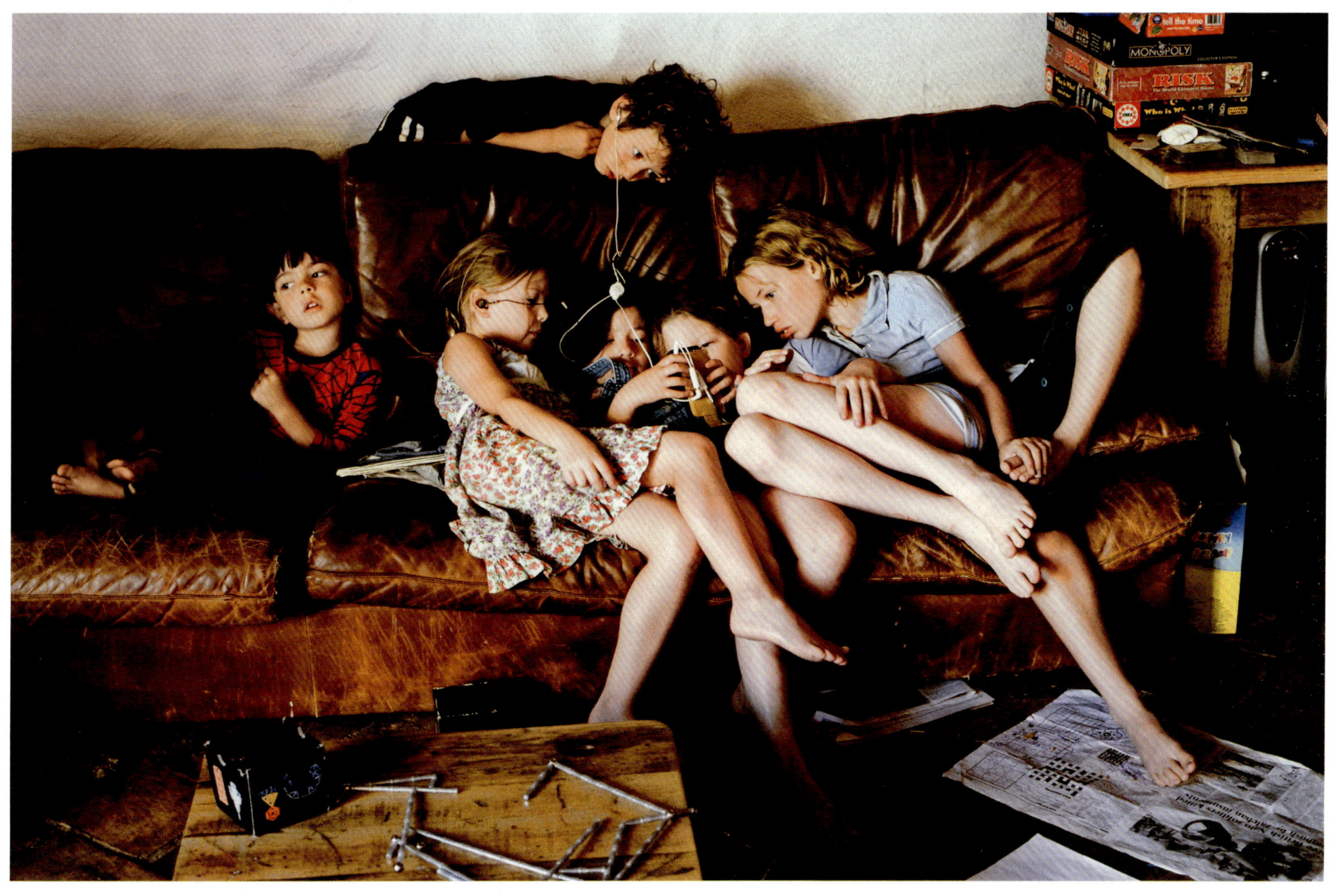

Ewan McNicol

Beautiful Birds
from the series
Pet Stories
June 2006

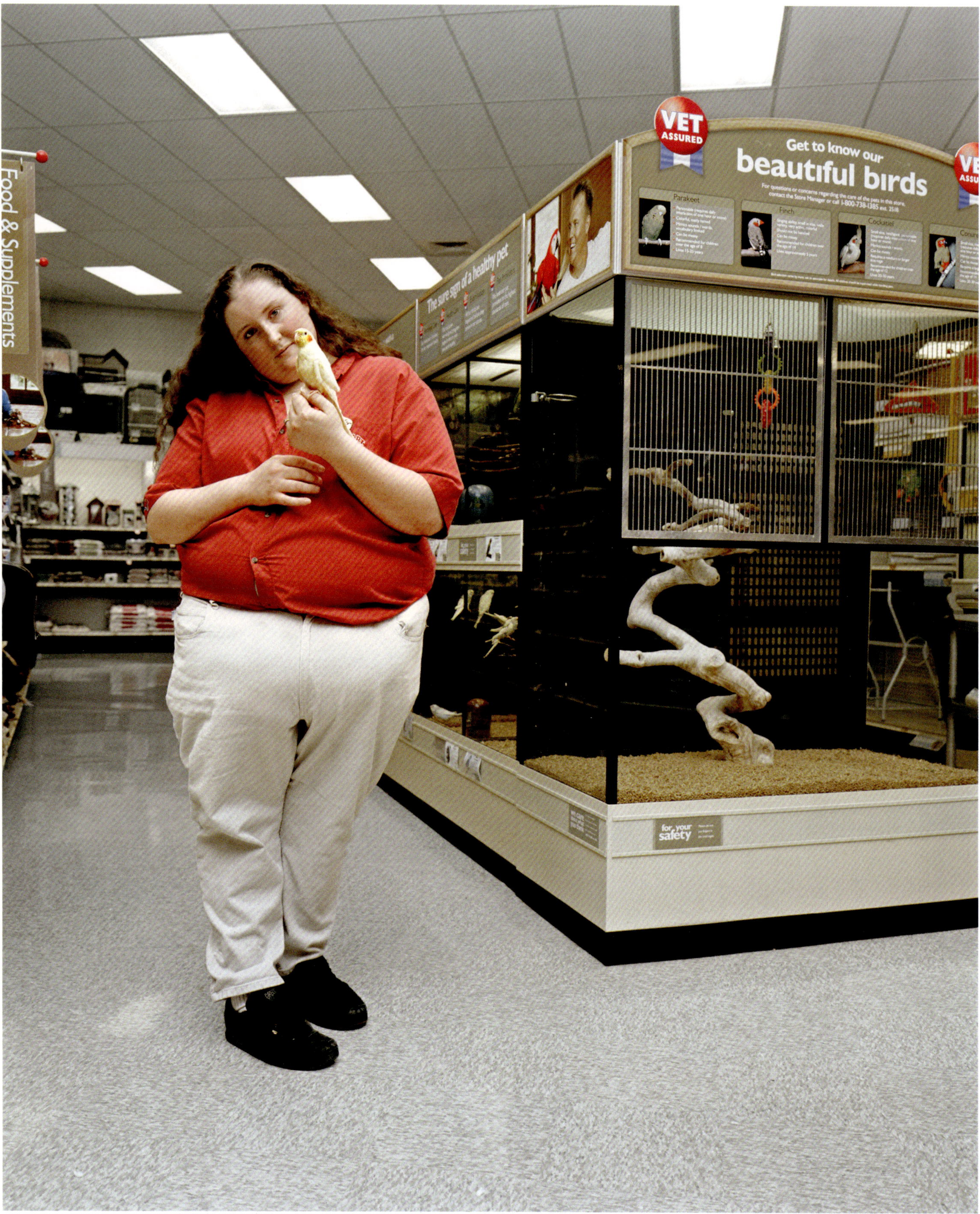

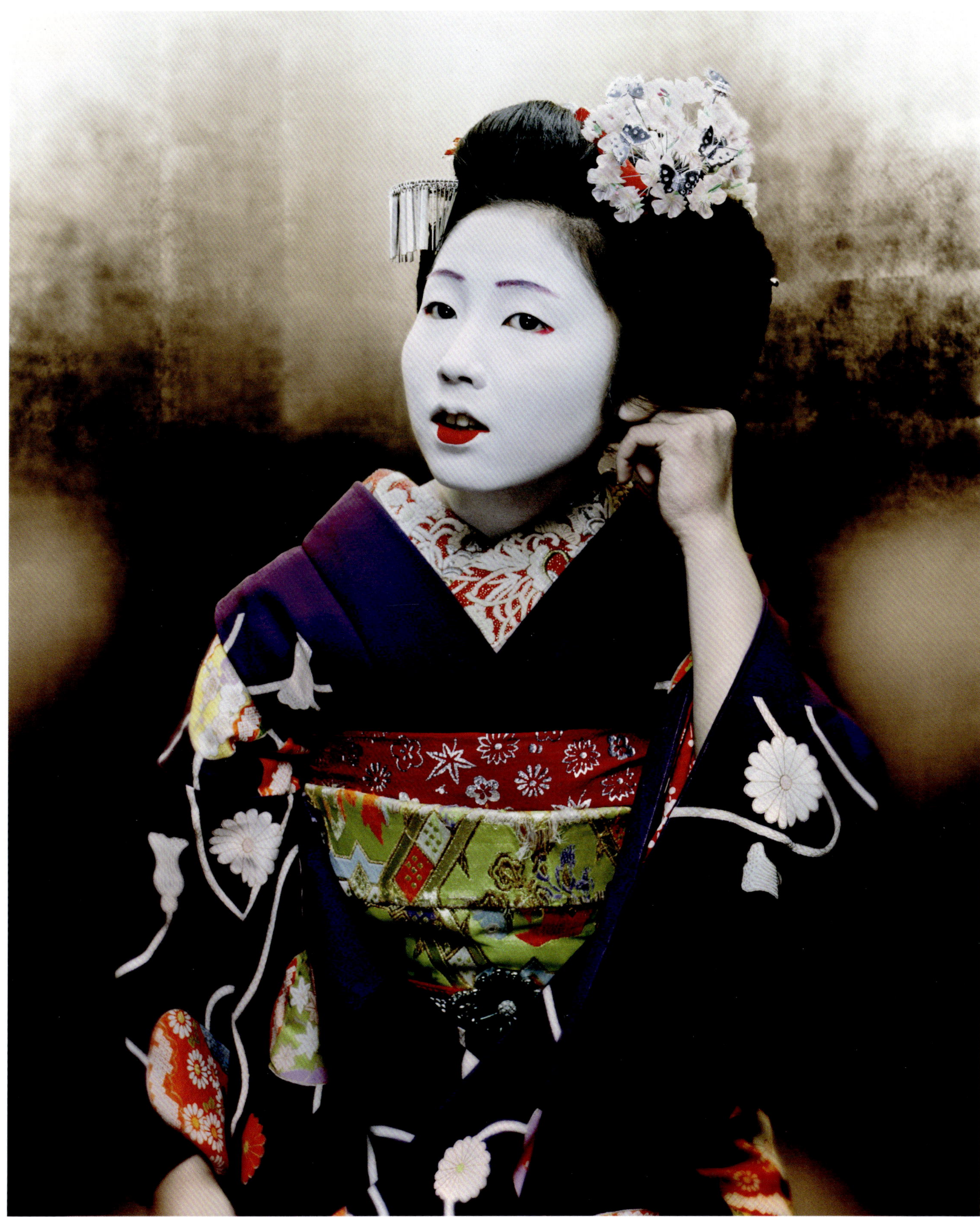

Denise Riley
December 2006

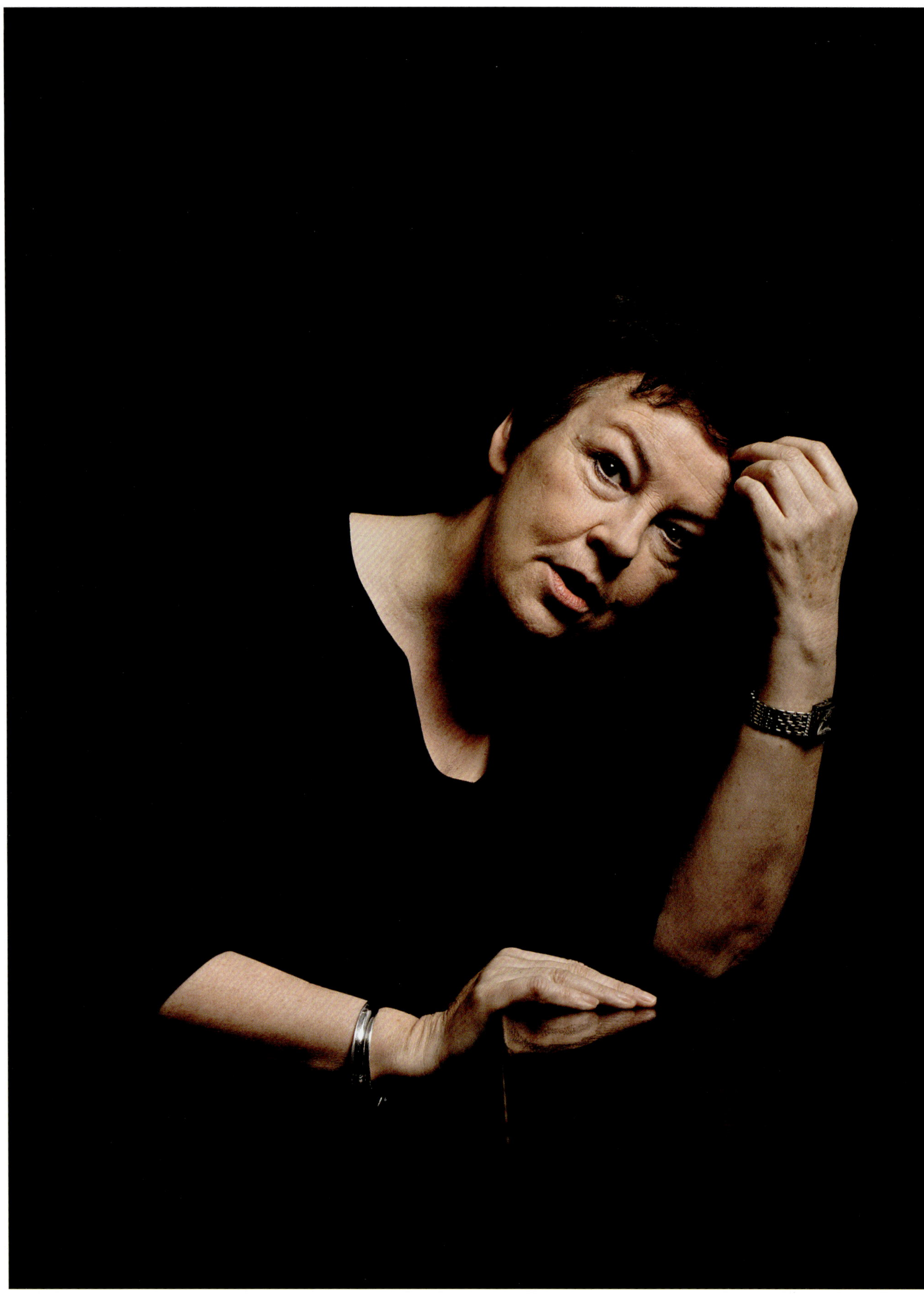

Veronique Rolland

Svenja und Nadine
from the series
Rothaarige Berlin
April 2007

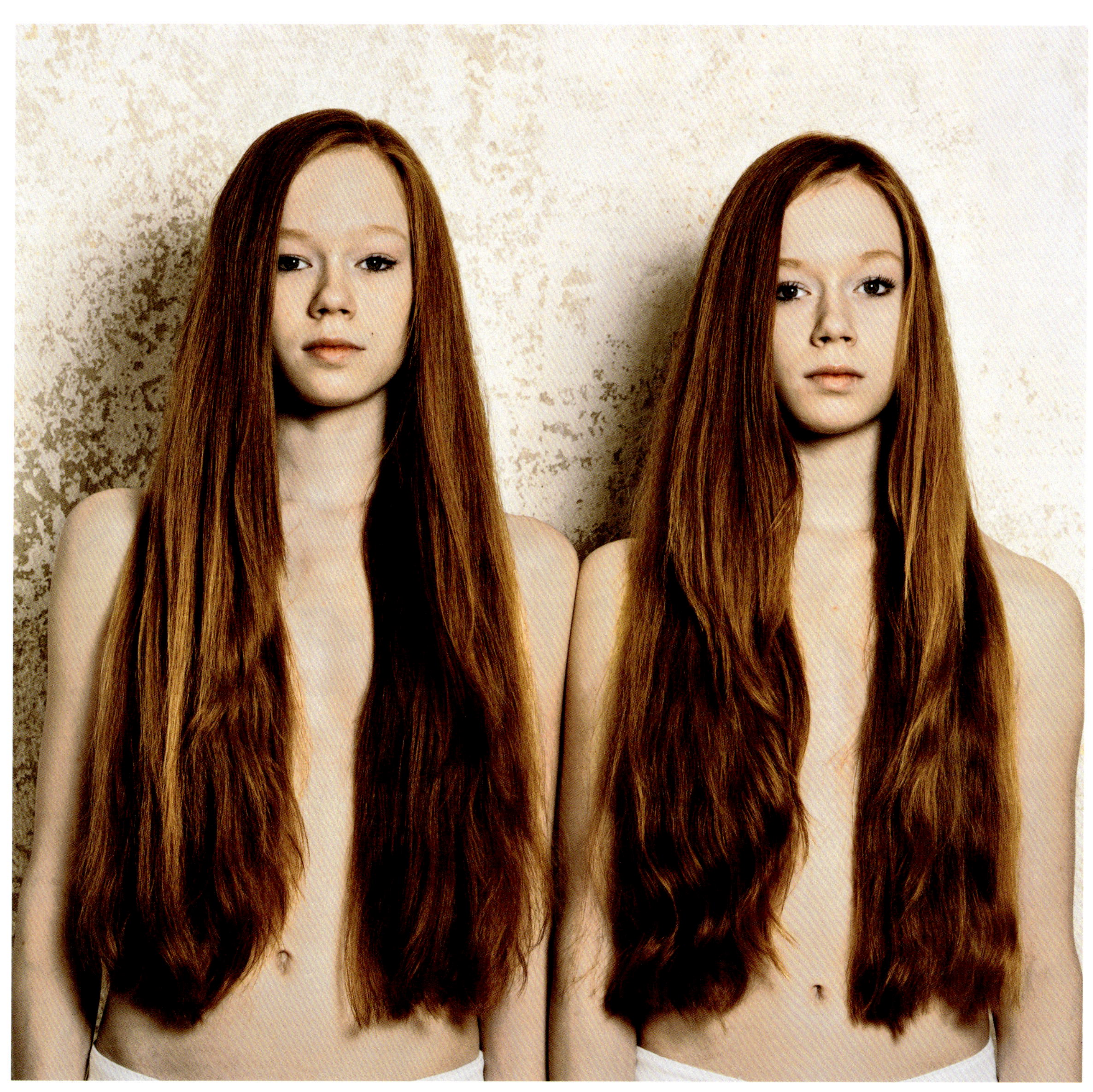

Colin Pantall

Sofa Portrait #3
from the series
Sofa
February 2006

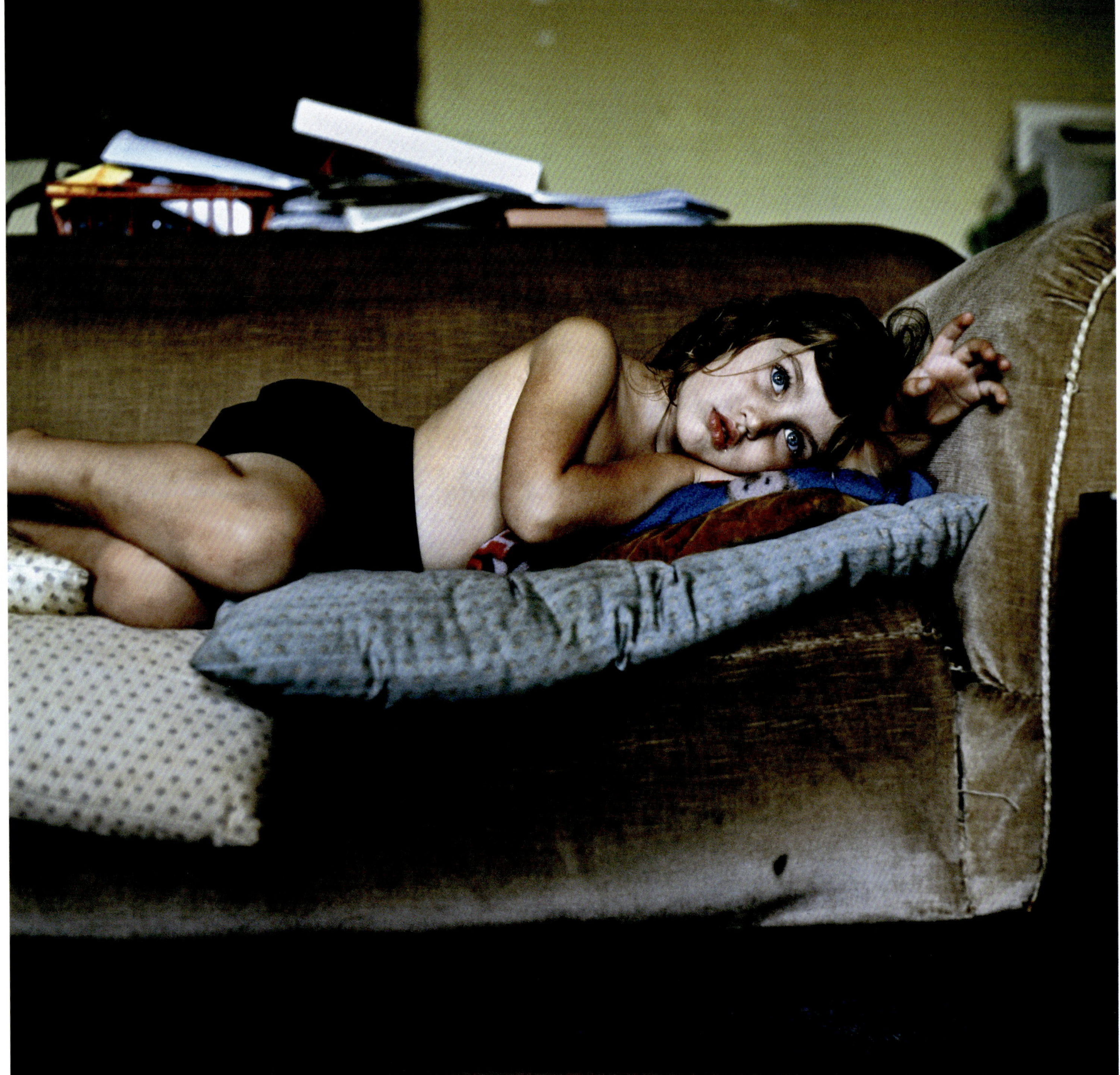

Sean Raggett

Fourth of July
(Wanting, Waiting)
July 2006

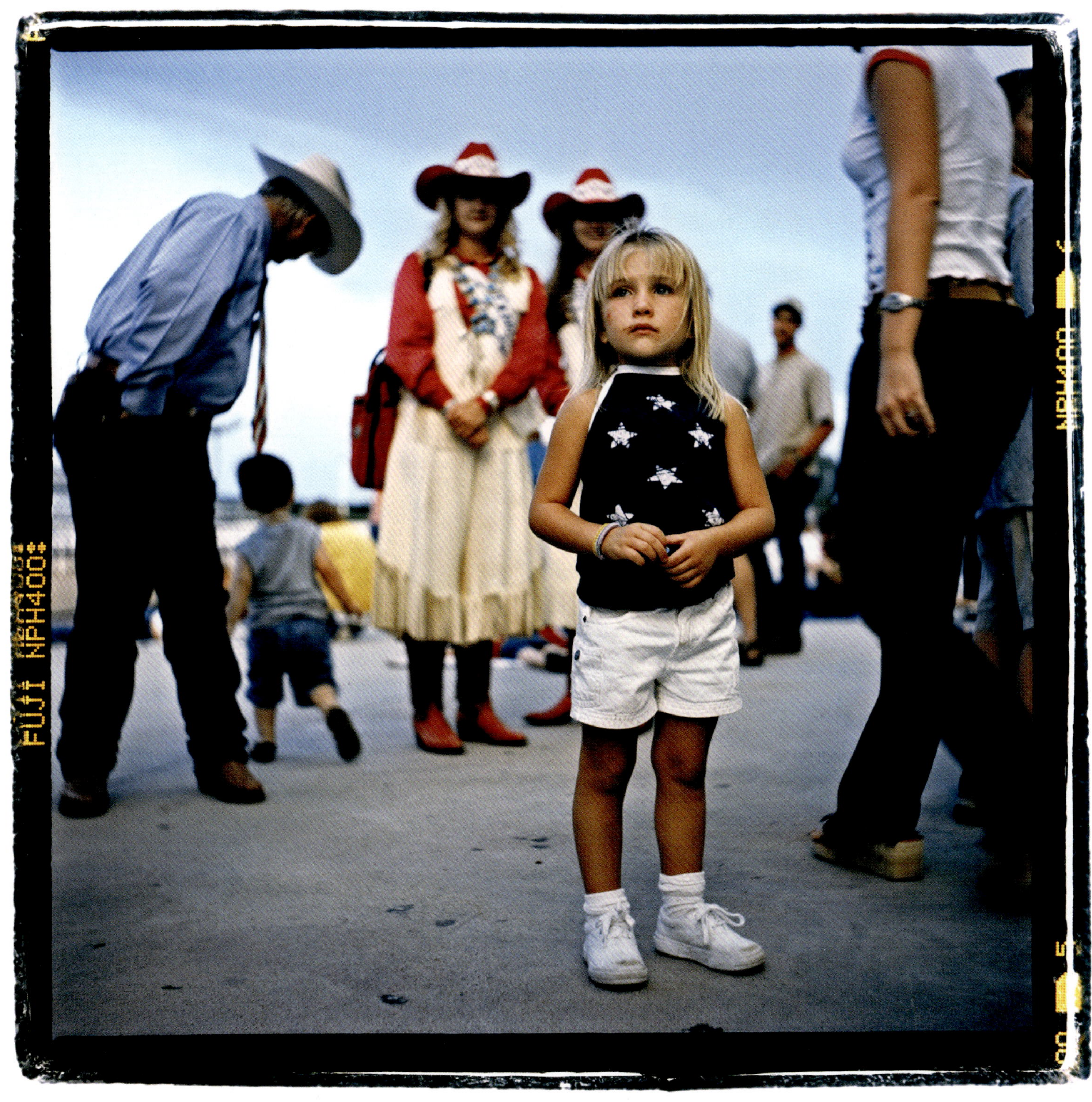

Colby Katz

Rayne-Lin, Little Miss Firecracker, LA *from the series* Darling May 2006

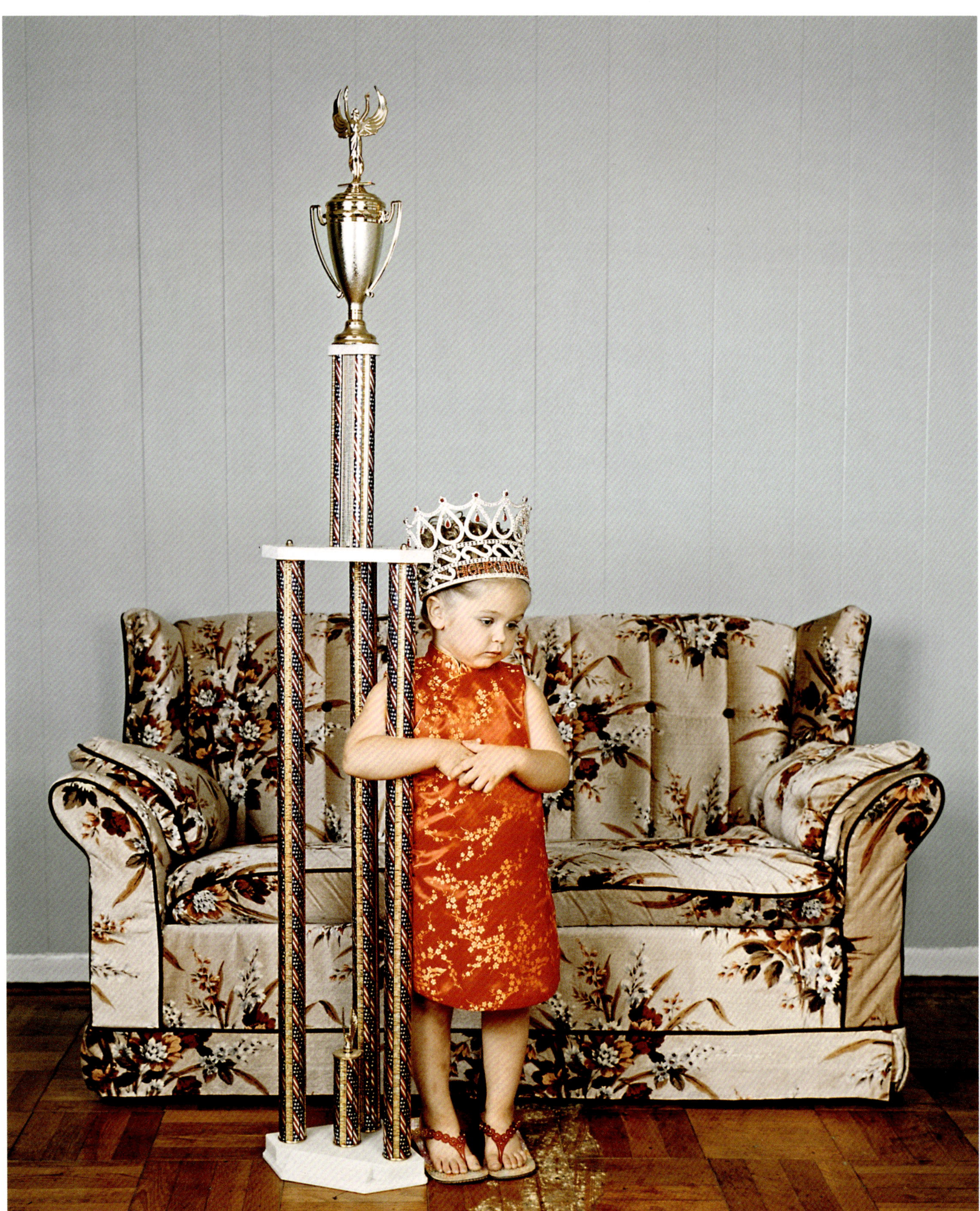

Anna
April 2006

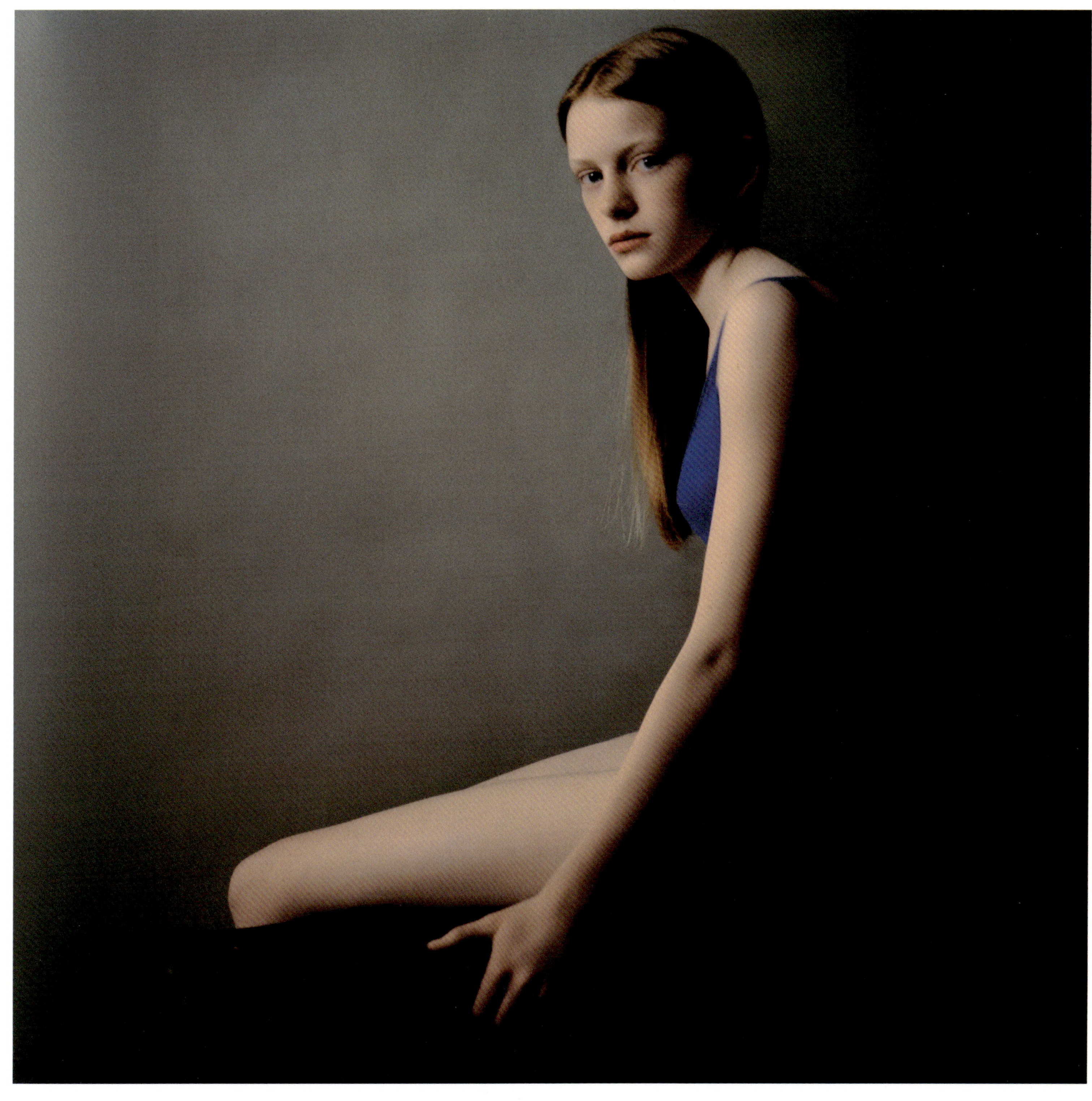

James O. Davies

Green Street Mosque, Iman
from the series

Places of Worship, Bristol
February 2007

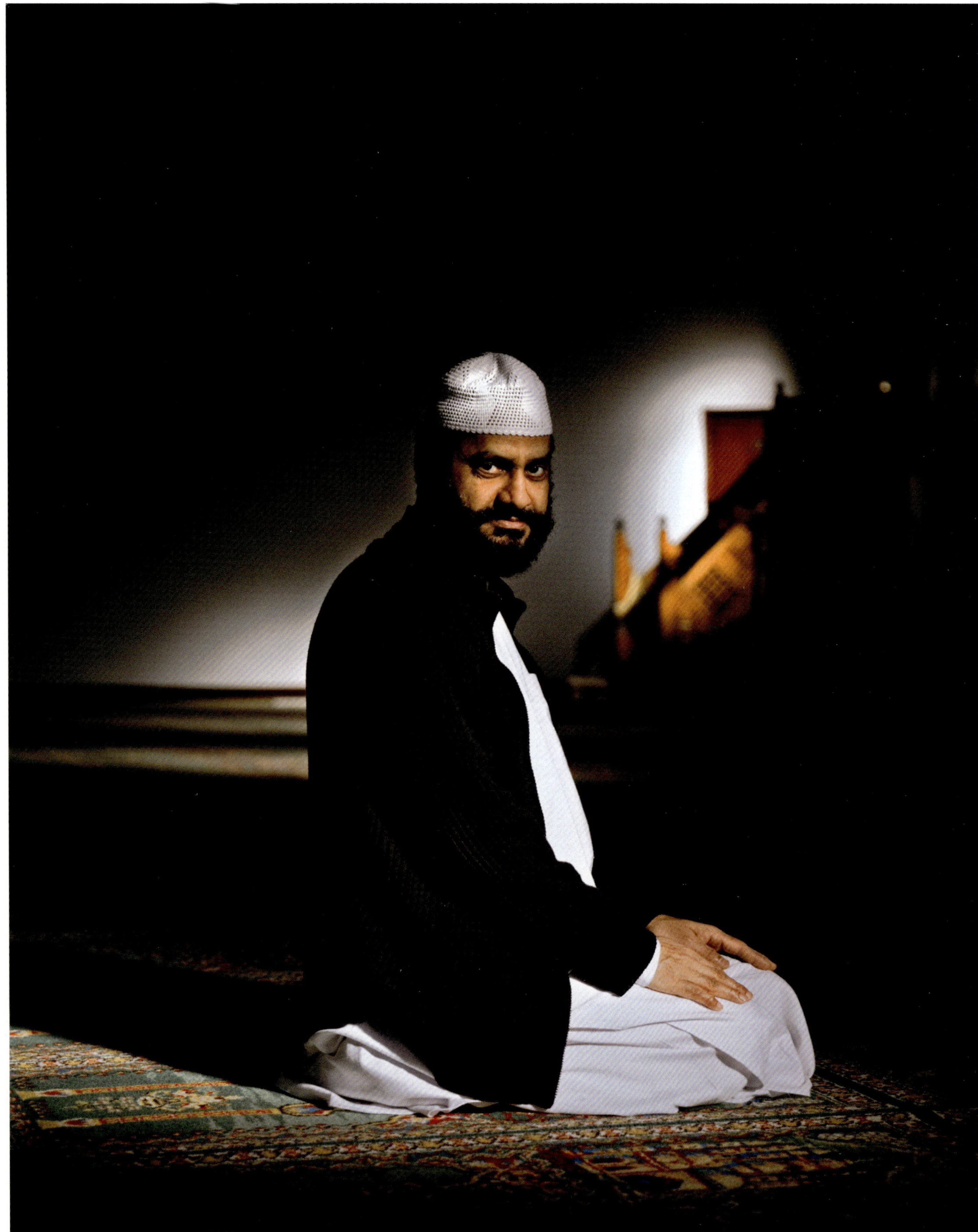

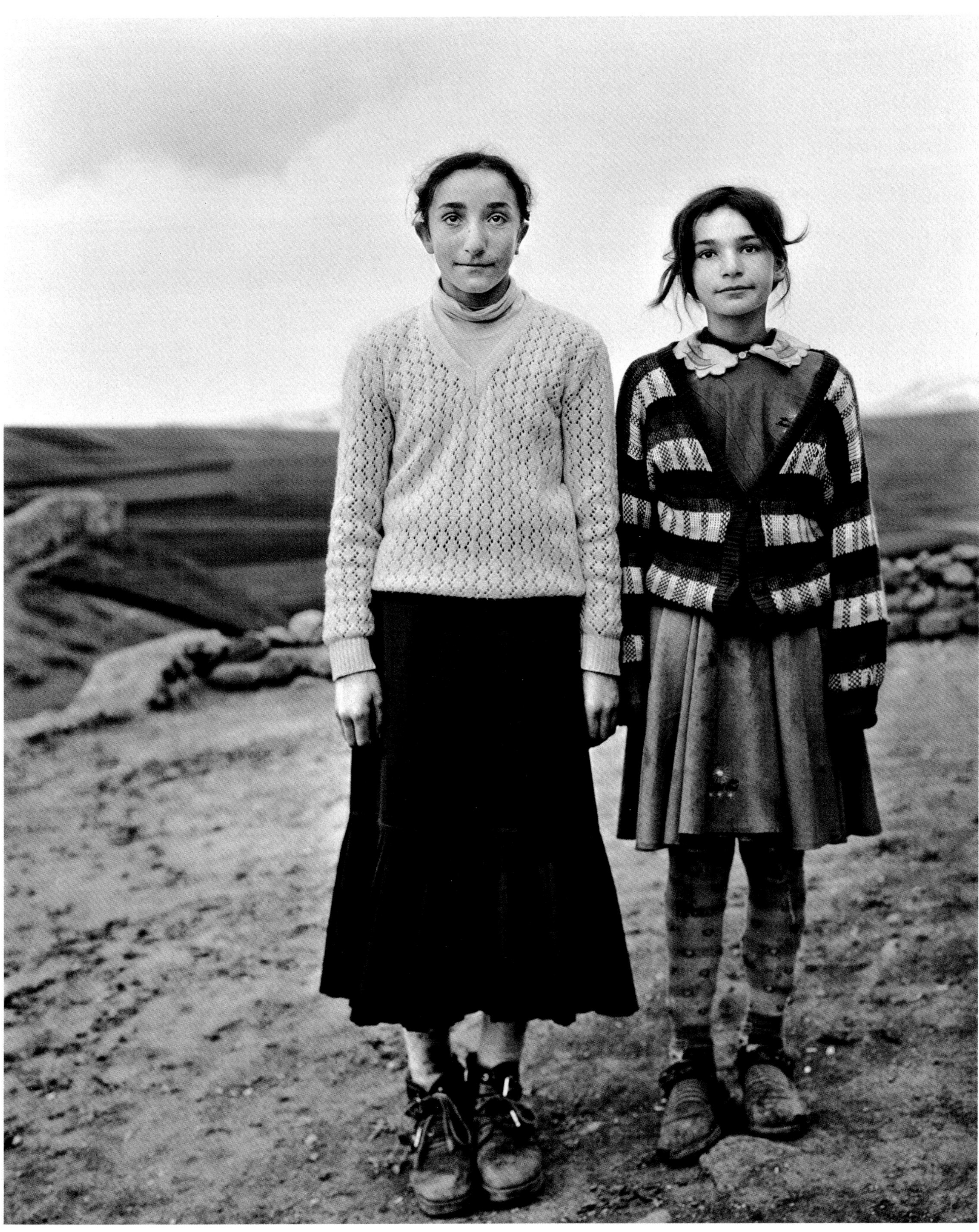

Brittany
May 2007

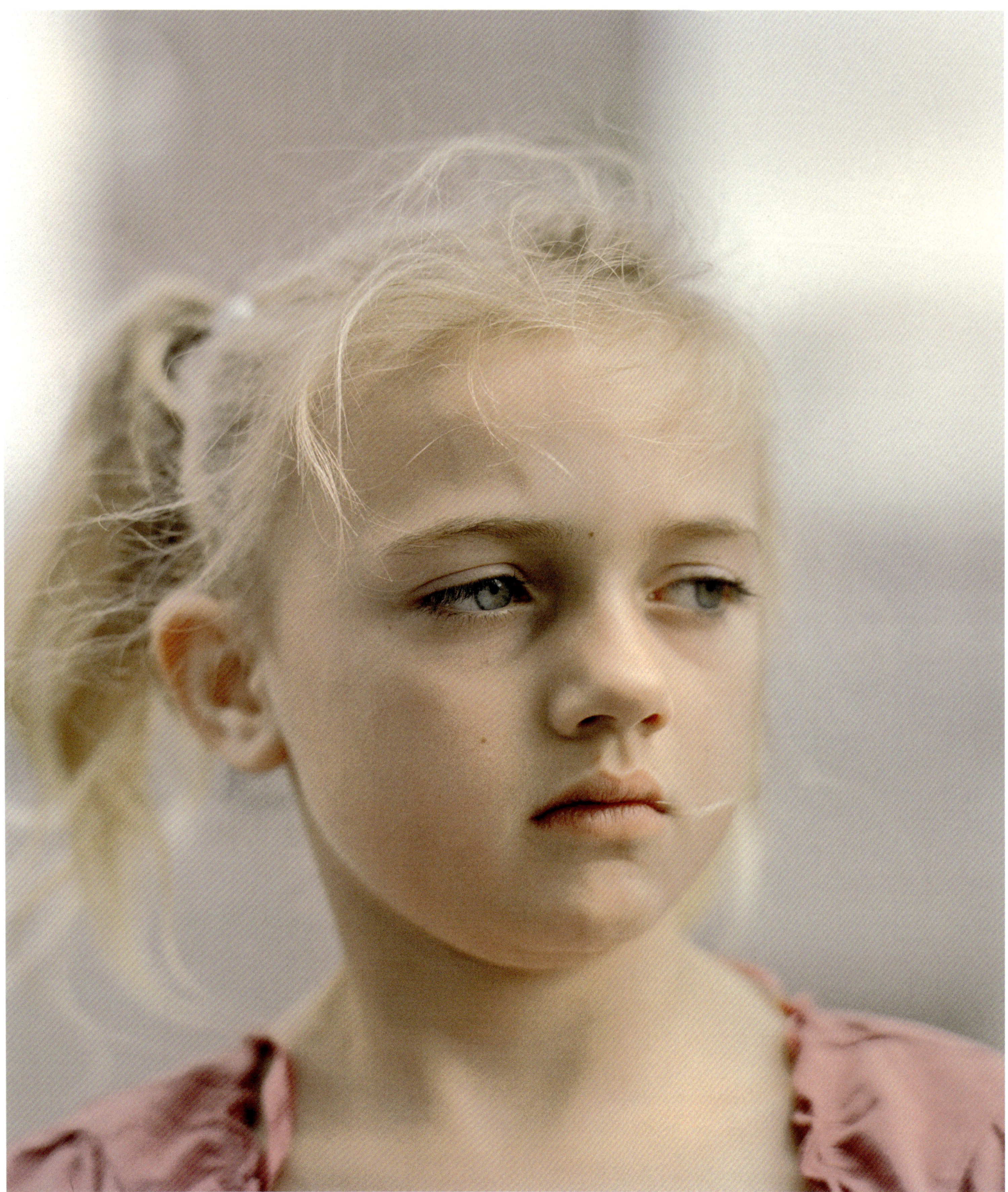

Leonie
July 2007

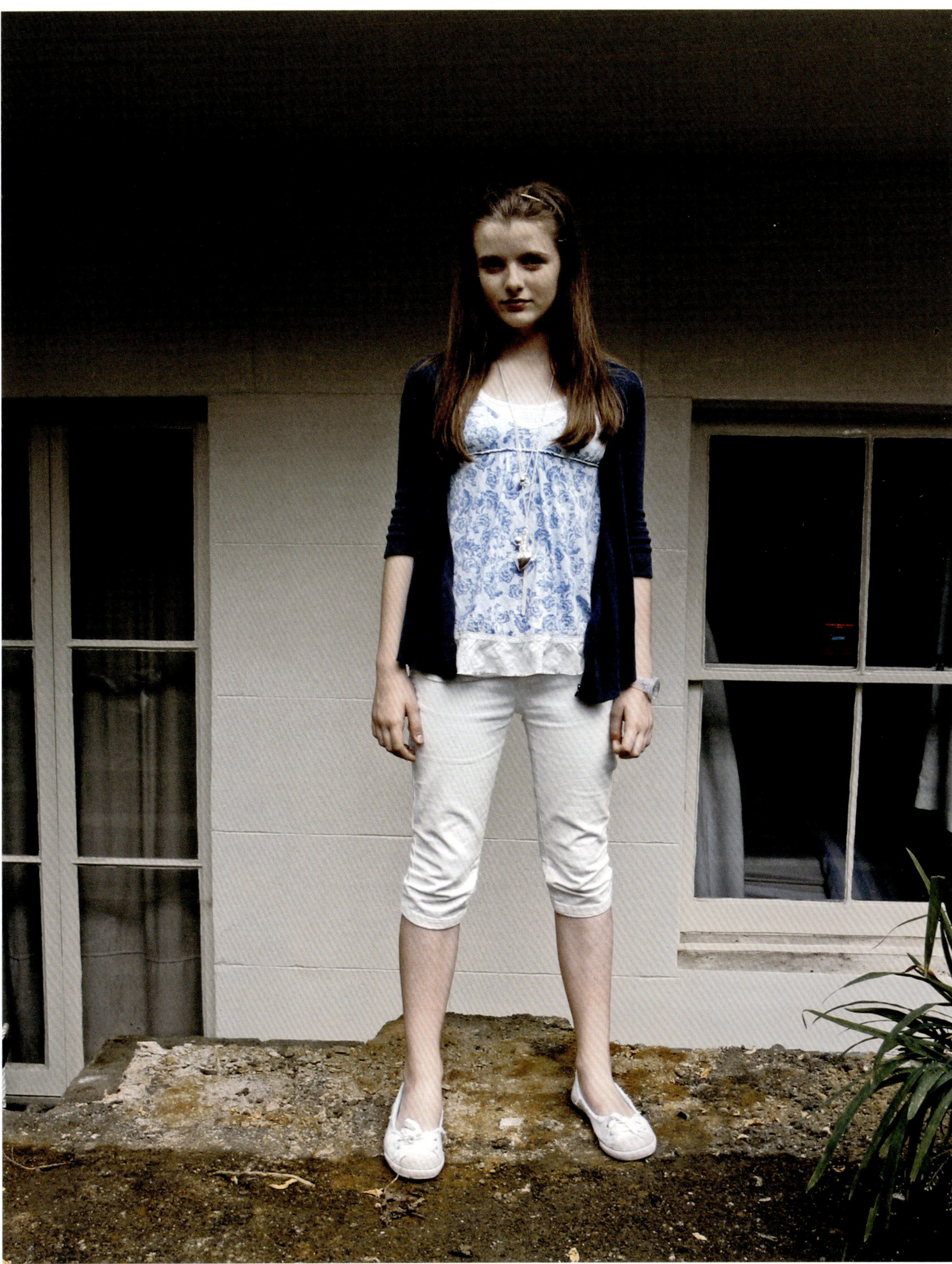

Justin Booth-Clibborn

Lydia's Bathroom
from the series
Home
February 2007

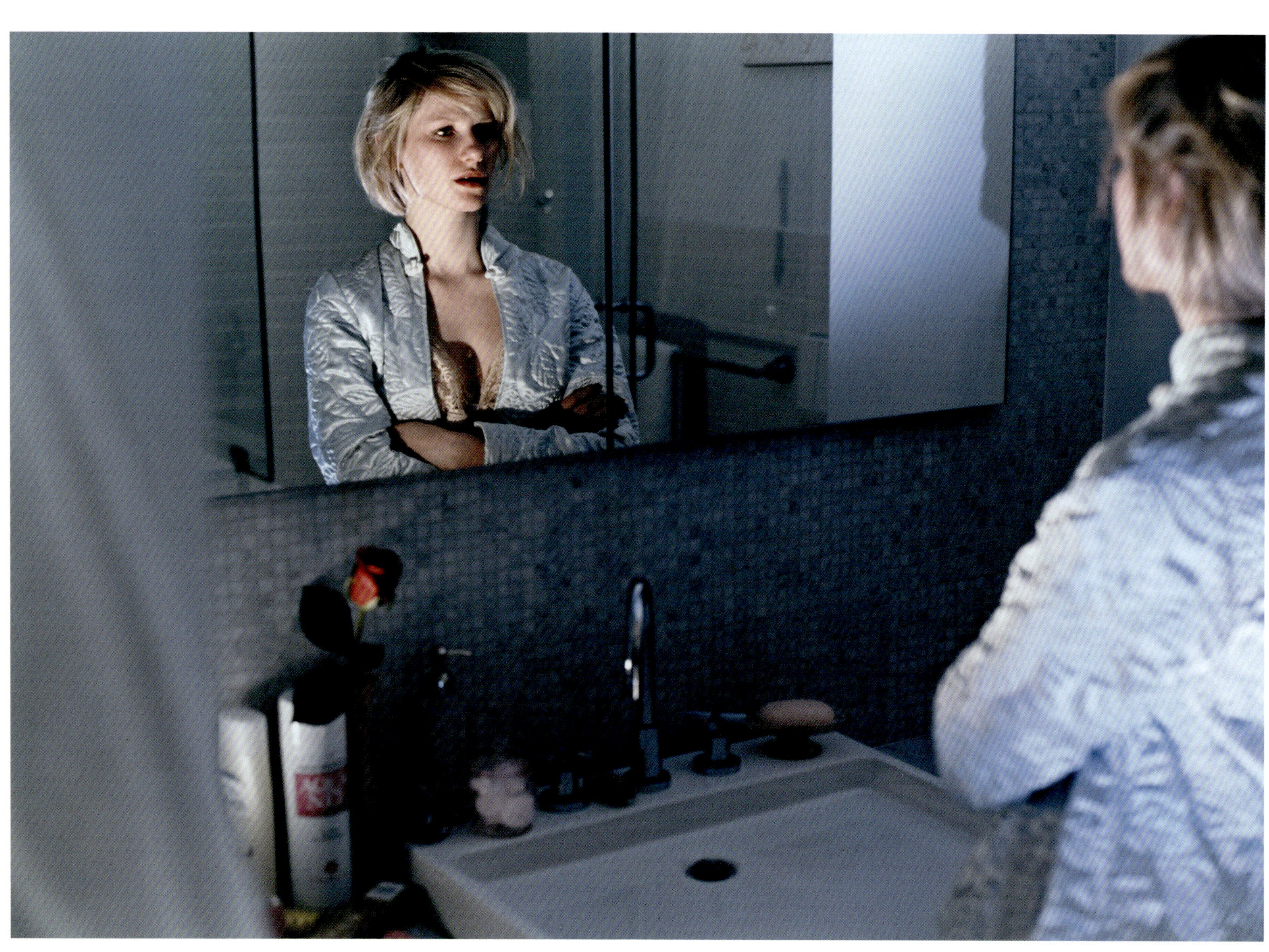

Laura Heyman

Untitled
from the series
The Photographer's
Wife
July 2006

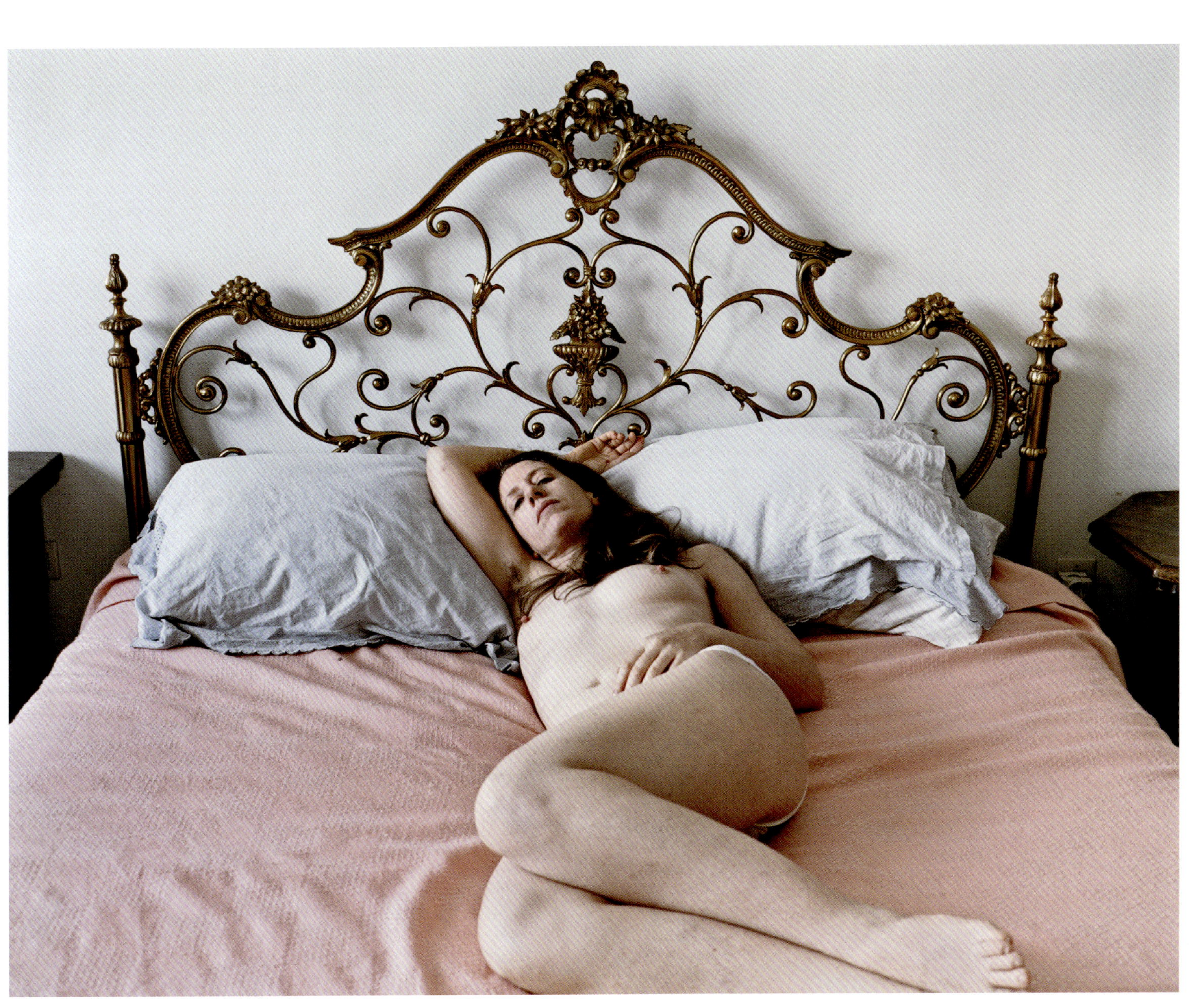

Luca J. Sage

Untitled
from the series

Wellington Balakasi
and other Portraits
May 2006

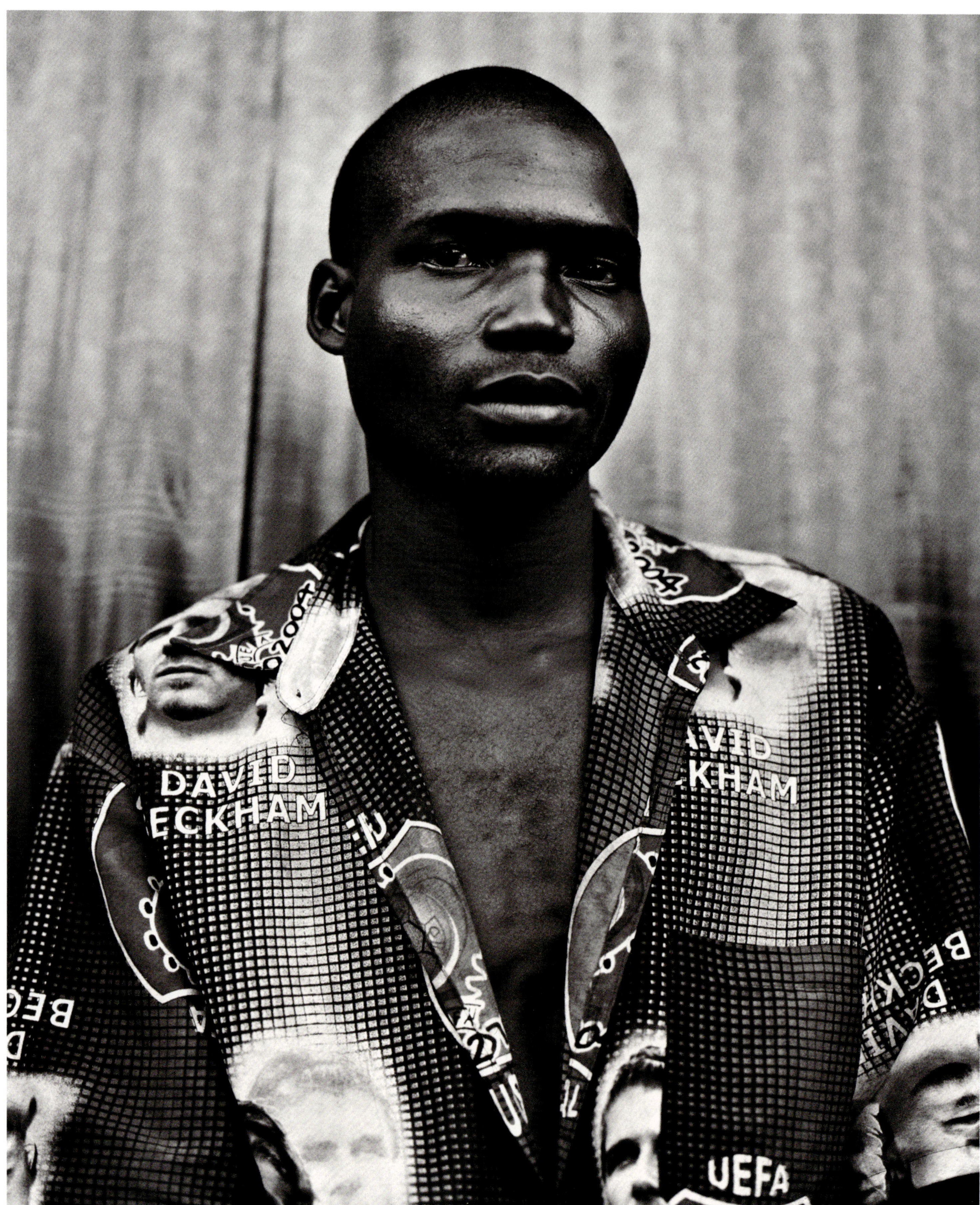

Sukey Parnell

Karen aka 'Dolly', Terminus Close, Brighton
from the series
Women of an Uncertain Age
June 2007

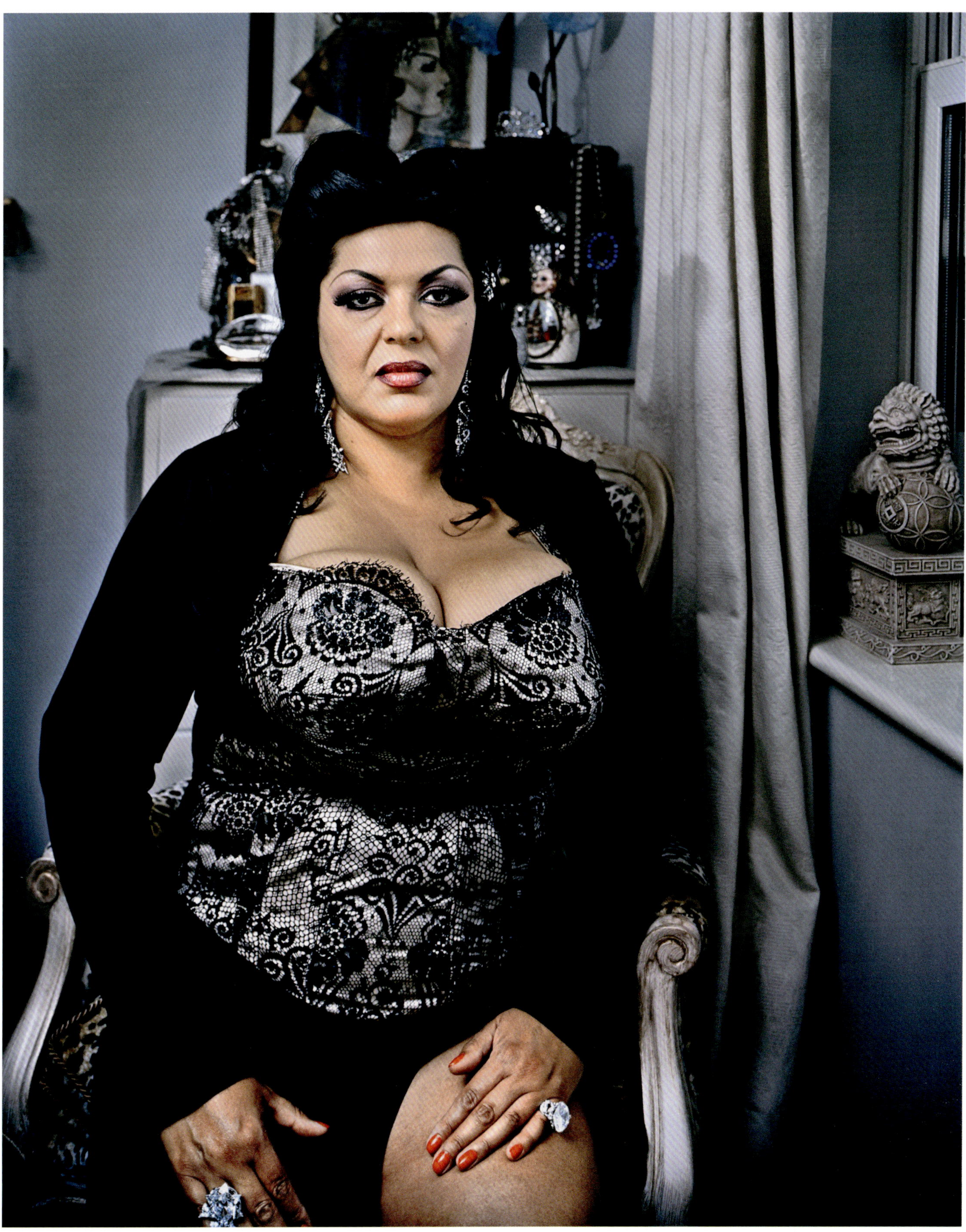

Three Russians
Visit Sweden
June 2006

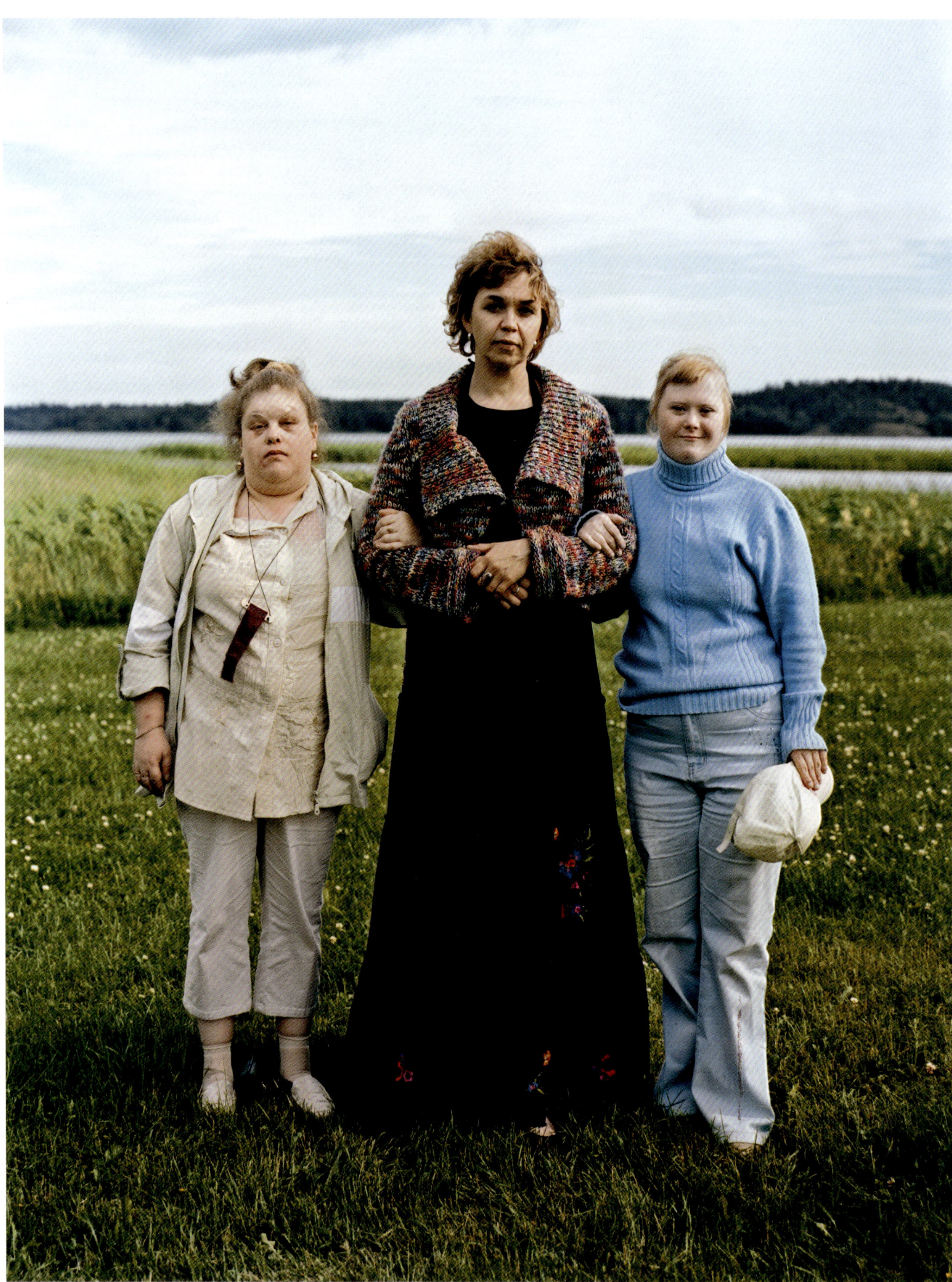

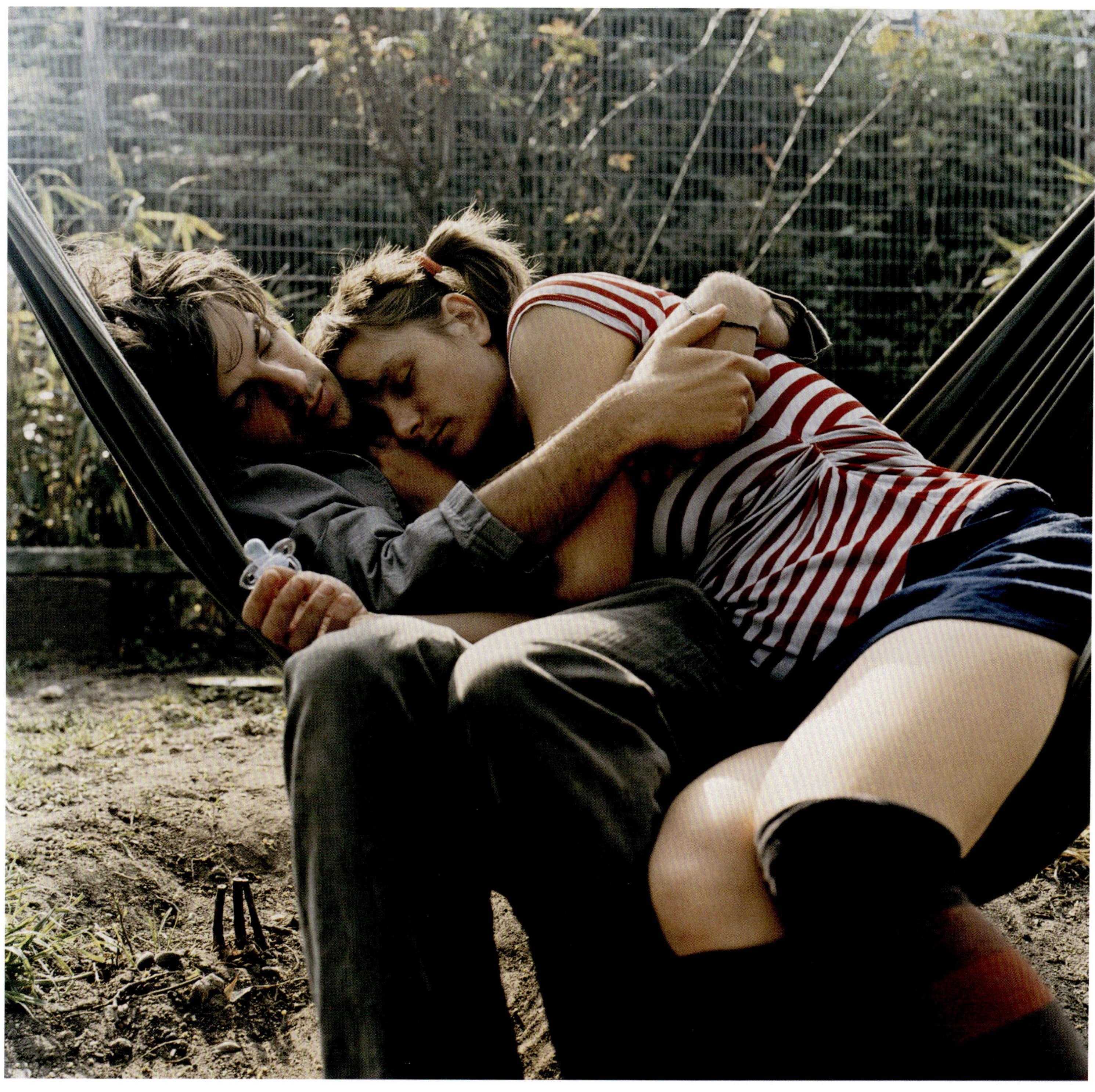

Charlie Crane

Ice Rink
June 2006

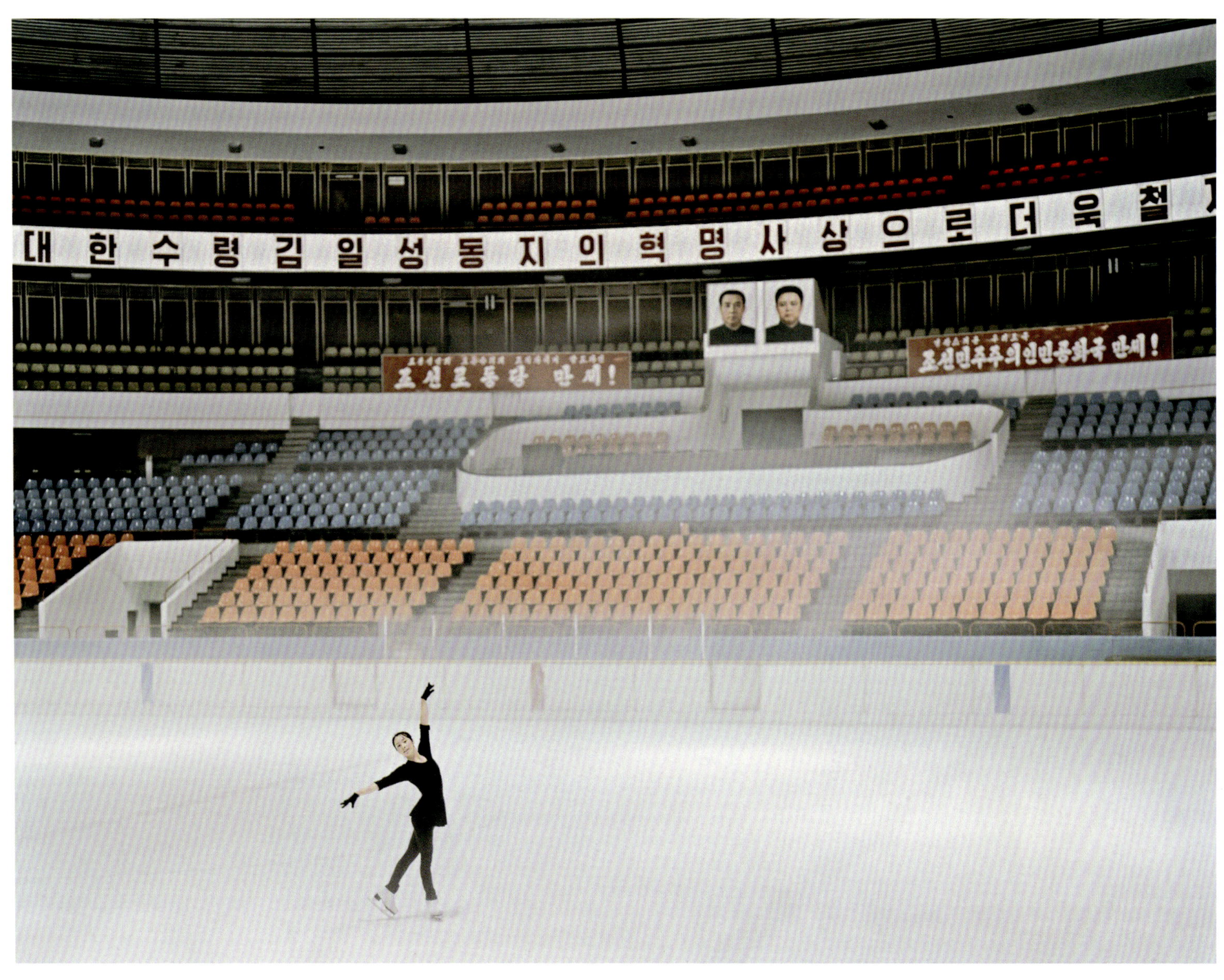

Richard Boll

Hiromi Yamaguchi
Migas
July 2007

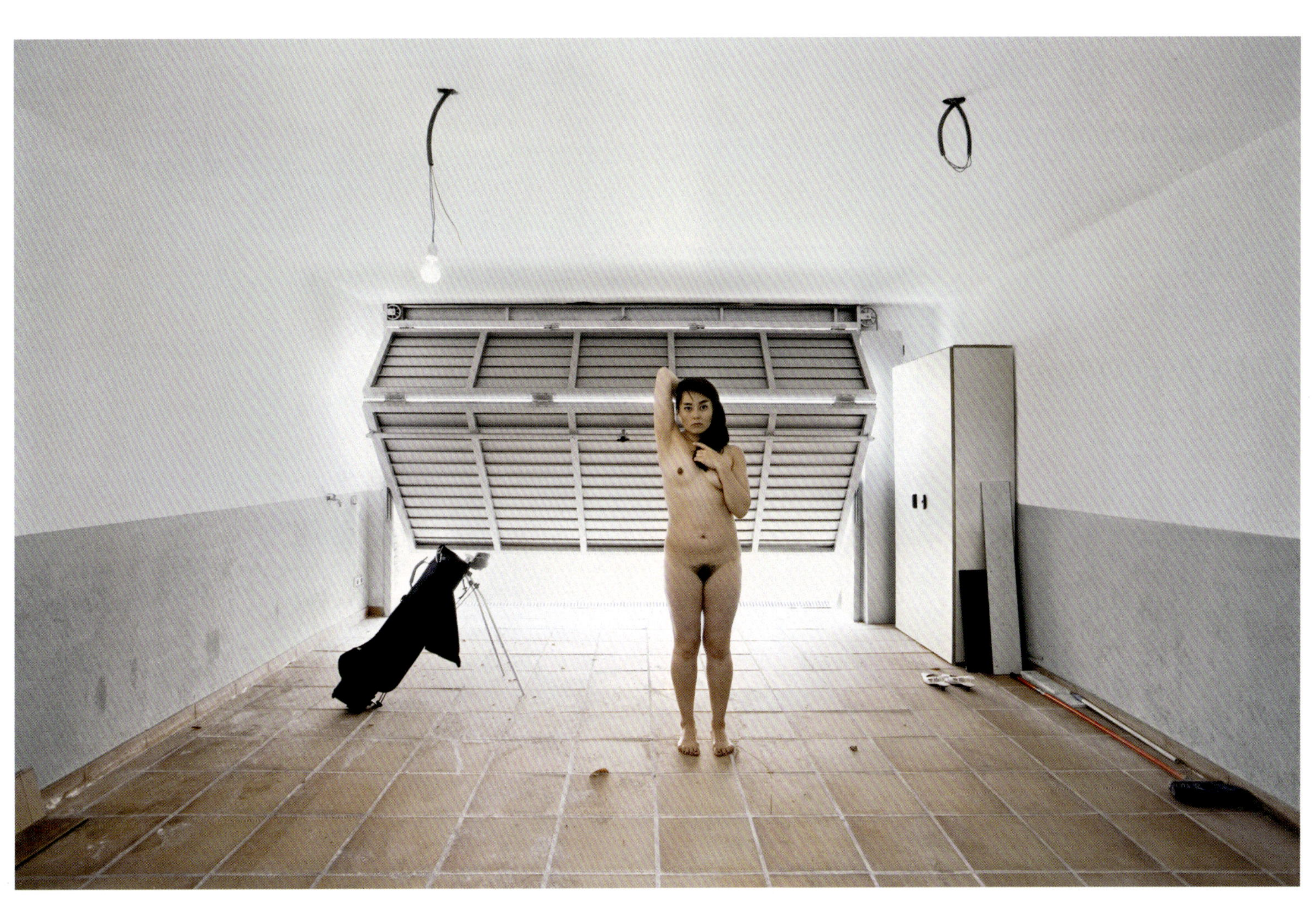

Sasha, UK
June 2007

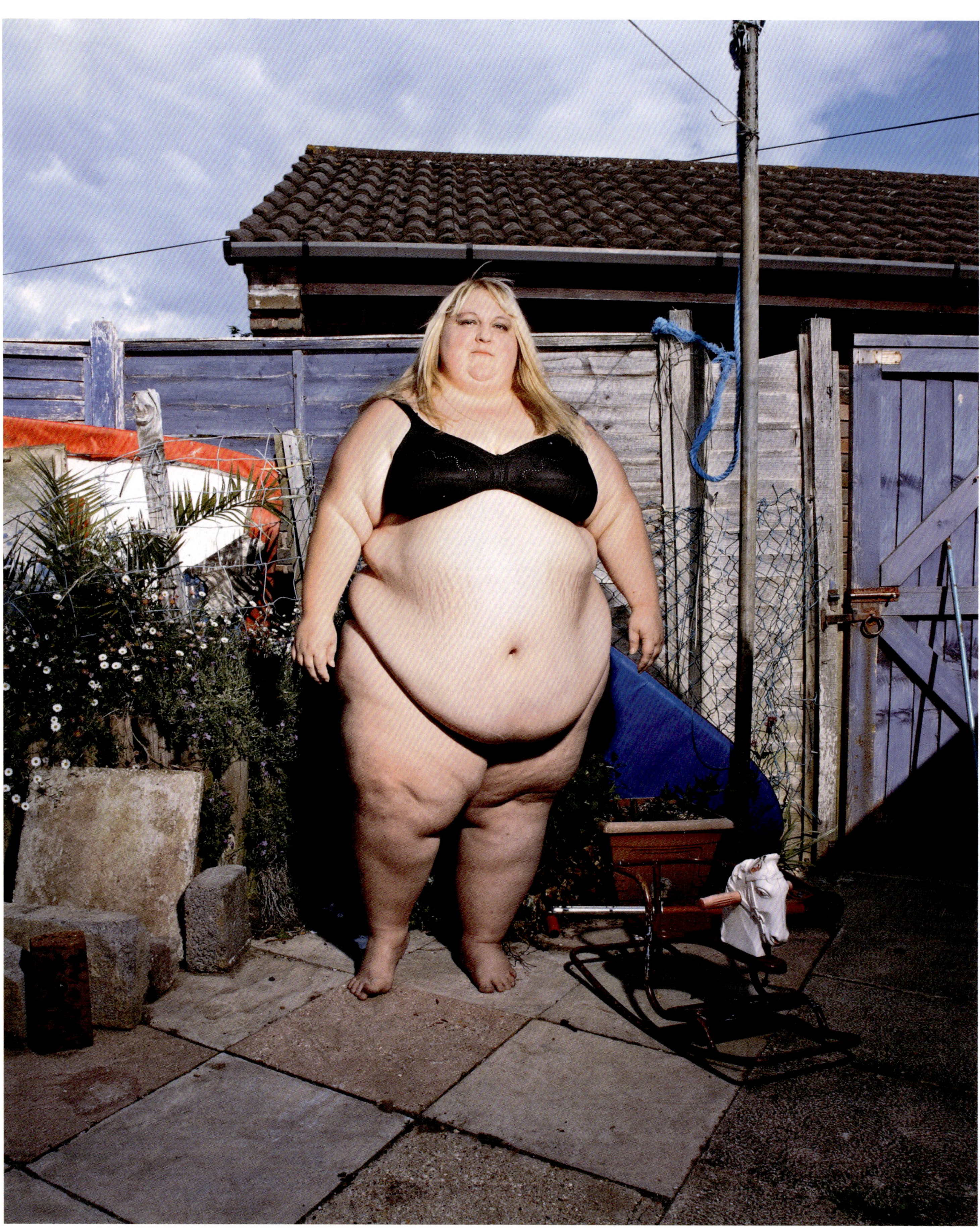

Dona Schwartz

Tammy and Jeremy,
7 Days
from the series
On the Nest
April 2007

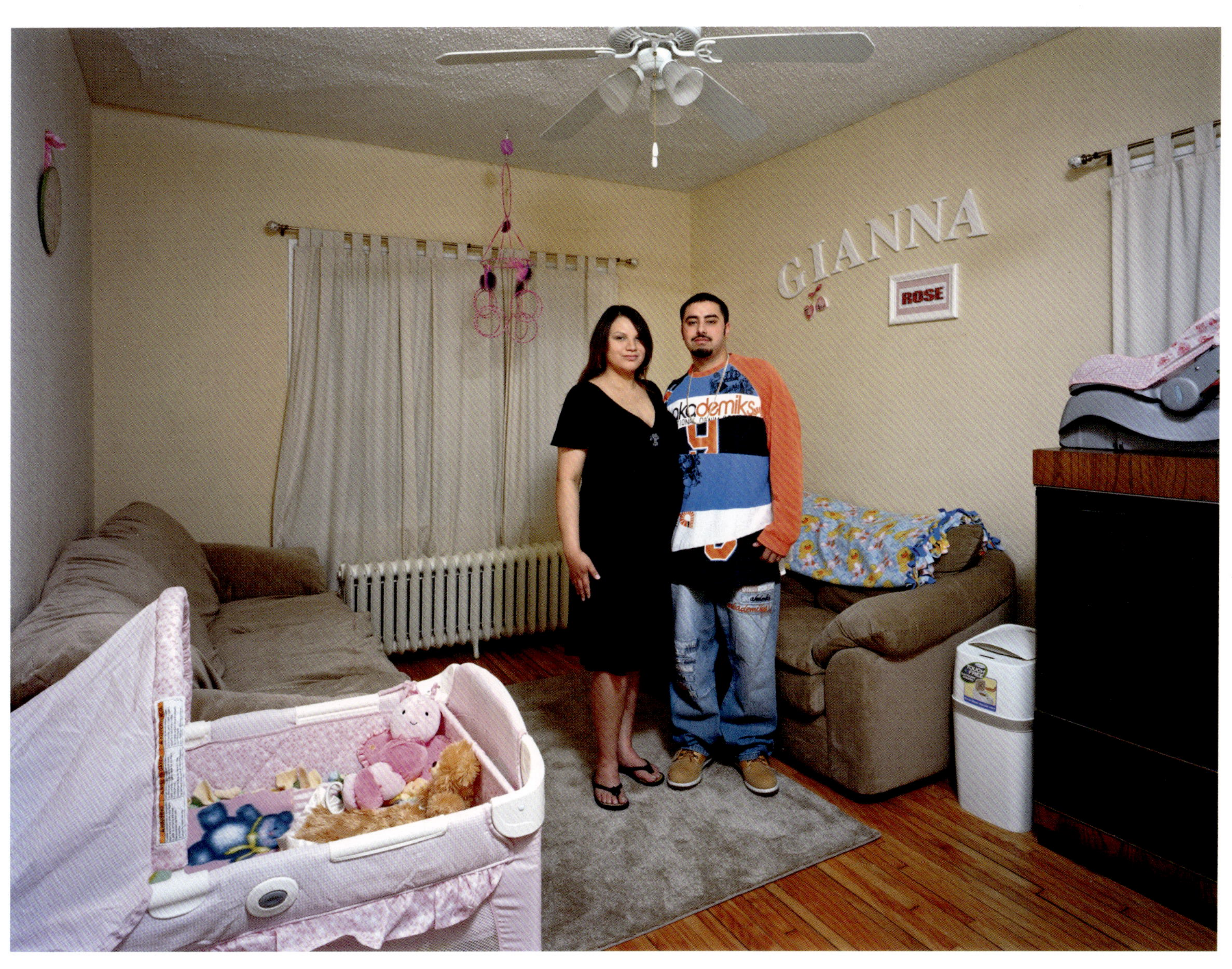

Susie Forman

Hogar Materno 1
from the series

Hogar Materno:
The Birth of a Nation
November 2006

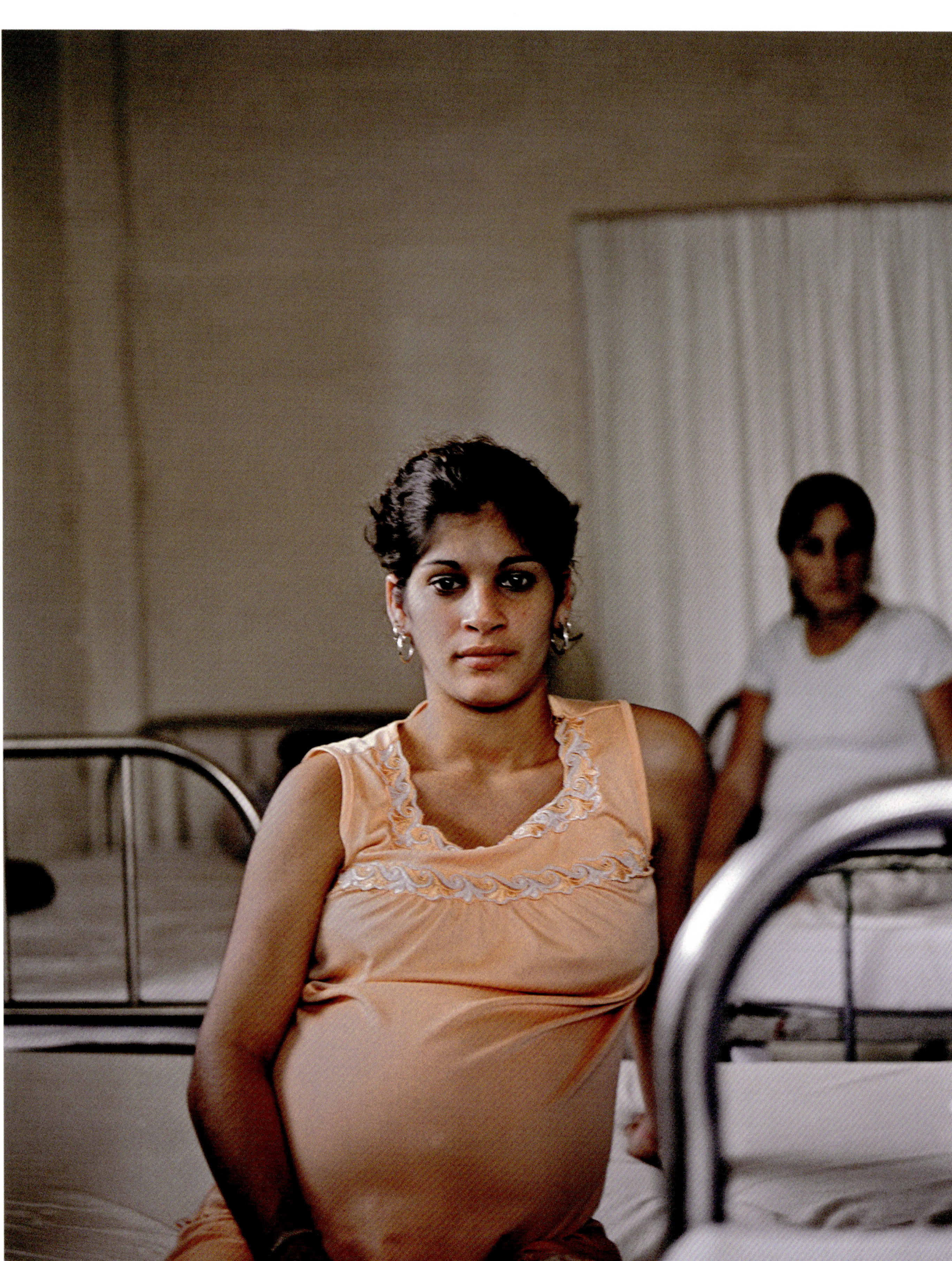

Jonathan Anderson and Edwin Low

Nataliya & Misha, Trapeze Artists *from the series*

Circus

August 2006

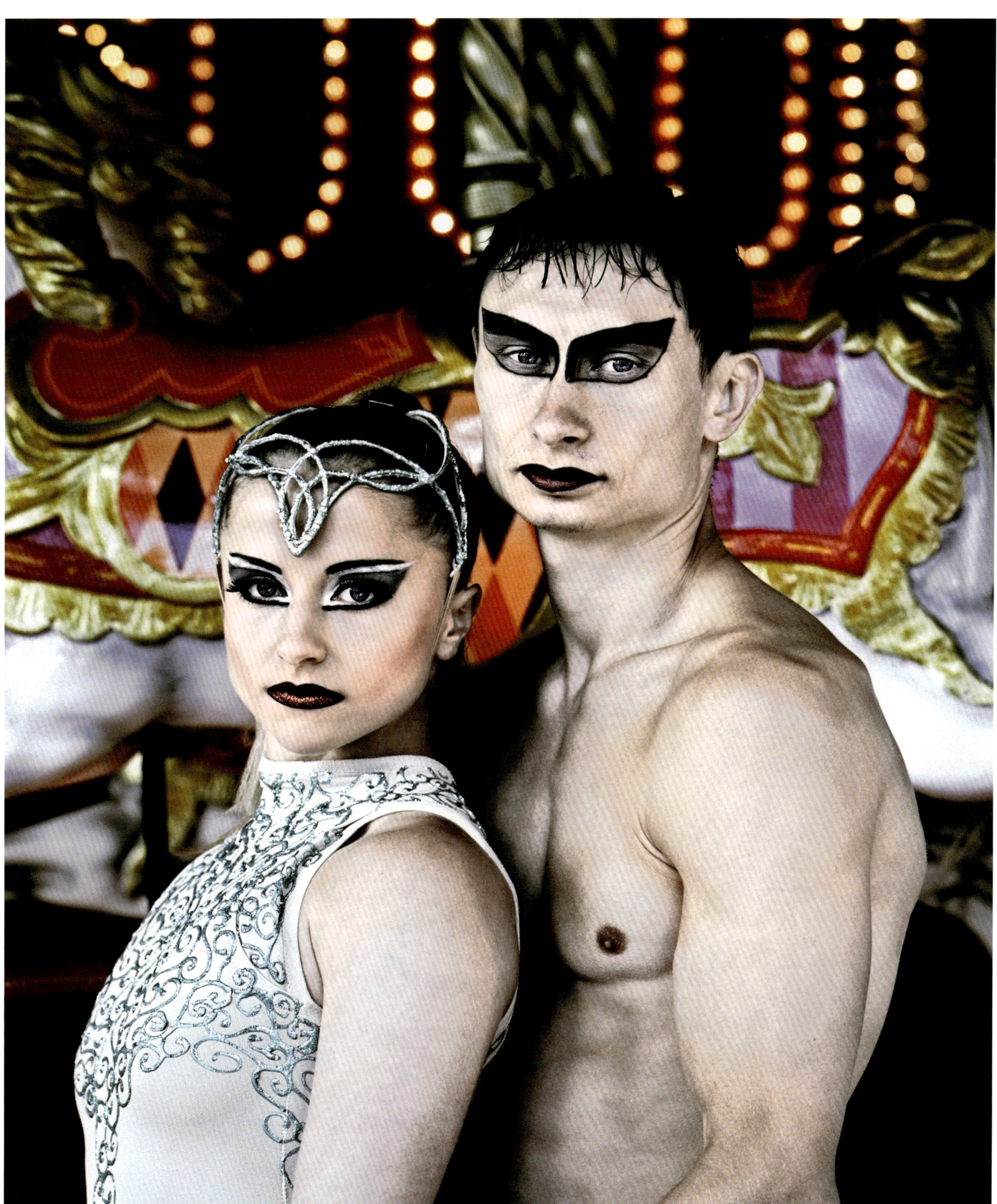

List of Exhibitors